LIVING LANGUAGE®

COMPLETE GUIDE TO
ARABIC
SCRIPT

Written by
Rym Bettaieb

Edited by
Christopher A. Warnasch

ACKNOWLEDGMENTS

Thanks to the Living Language team: Tom Russell, Nicole Benhabib, Christopher Warnasch, Zviezdana Verzich, Suzanne McQuade, Shaina Malkin, Elham Shabahat, Sophie Chin, Denise DeGennaro, Linda Schmidt, Alison Skrabek, Lisbeth Dyer, and Tom Marshall.

Special thanks to Wafaa H. Wahba for his valuable contribution, and also to Daniel Doyle, Michael B. Francis, and Michelle Saks.

DEDICATION

To my first Arabic teacher, Madame Haami.

الكتاب إلى من علمتني اللغة العربية، السيدة حامي

www.livinglanguage.com

Editor: Christopher Warnasch
Production Editor: Lisbeth Dyer
Production Manager: Tom Marshall
Interior Design: Sophie Chin

First Edition
ISBN: 978-1-4000-0924-4

Library of Congress Cataloging-in-Publication Data available upon request.

This book is available at special discounts for bulk purchases for sales promotions or premiums. Special editions, including personalized covers, excerpts of existing books, and corporate imprints, can be created in large quantities for special needs. For more information, write to Special Markets/Premium Sales, 1745 Broadway, MD 6-2, New York, New York 10019 or e-mail specialmarkets@randomhouse.com.

PRINTED IN THE UNITED STATES OF AMERICA
10 9 8 7 6 5 4 3 2 1

TABLE OF CONTENTS

Introduction v

Arabic Courses Offered by Living Language ix

PART 1: Pronunciation and Transcription 1

Vowels 3

Consonants 6

Group 1: Sounds that are similar to English 7

Group 2: Sounds that are similar to other European languages 12

Group 3: Unfamiliar sounds 14

PART 2: Reading Arabic 19

The basics 19

The Arabic alphabet 19

Connecting and non-connecting letters 24

Group 1: Long vowels 25

Group 2: Short vowels and diphthongs 25

Group 3: ب b, ت t, and ث th 27

Group 4: ج j, ح H, and خ kh 29

Group 5: د d, ذ dh, ر r, and ز z 30

Group 6: س s and ش sh 33

Group 7: ص S, ض D, ط T, and ظ DH 34

Group 8: ع x and غ gh 36

Group 9: ف f and ق q 38

Group 10: ك k, ل l, م m, and ن n 39

Group 11: ‎ه h and **taa' marbuuTa** 41

Group 12: **shadda, laam-'alif,** and the definite article 45

13: **hamza** 49

14: **'alif maqSuura** 53

15: Grammatical endings with -**n** 54

16: Other symbols 56

PART 3: Writing Arabic 60

Group 1: Long vowels 60

Group 2: Short vowels and diphthongs 63

Group 3: ب, ت, and ث 65

Group 4: ج, ح, and خ 69

Group 5: د, ذ, ر, and ز 73

Group 6: س and ش 79

Group 7: ص, ض, ط, and ظ 82

Group 8: ع and غ 86

Group 9: ف and ق 89

Group 10: ك, ل, م, and ن 92

Group 11: ه and ة 97

Group 12: **shadda, laam-'alif,** and the definite article 101

13: **hamza** 103

14: **'alif maqSuura** and grammatical endings with -**n** 106

PART 4: Reading Passages 111

Dialogue 1 111

Dialogue 2 113

Dialogue 3 117

Dialogue 4 122

Introduction

The *Living Language Complete Guide to Arabic Script* is a beginner's course in reading and writing Arabic. It may be used as a supplement to any Arabic course, including *Living Language Complete Arabic: The Basics, Living Language Starting Out in Arabic,* or *Living Language Ultimate Arabic.* This book does not assume any background knowledge of Arabic, although since it focuses on reading and writing Arabic, it is most useful when used in conjunction with one of these courses, which teach everything you need to speak and understand Arabic.

Since Arabic uses a different script, students of the language need to make a choice as to when they'd like to tackle it. You may wish to focus first on the spoken language and develop skills in conversational Arabic before dealing with the written language. Or, you may prefer to focus on the two concurrently. The choice really depends on your needs and goals, so Living Language offers a range of Arabic courses. *Complete Arabic: The Basics* and *Starting Out in Arabic* are designed for students who prefer to focus on the spoken language first, and *Ultimate Arabic* is designed for students who prefer to learn both the written and the spoken language from the beginning. For a description of each of these programs and suggestions on how to use this book with them, see the section on *Arabic Courses Offered by Living Language,* which follows this introduction.

The *Complete Guide to Arabic Script* is divided into four parts: Pronunciation and Transcription, Reading Arabic, Writing Arabic, and Reading Passages.

PART 1: PRONUNCIATION AND TRANSCRIPTION

The first part of this book is designed to give the student a foundation in Arabic pronunciation, so that reading and writing will be less challenging. It uses a simple, intuitive transcription system. It presents each sound in Modern Standard Arabic, starting with vowels and then moving on to consonants, which are divided into three groups to make learning as easy as possible. The first group deals with sounds that are very similar in Arabic and English. The second group deals with sounds that are not part of standard English, but which will probably be familiar to many English speakers because they are found in other European languages. The third group covers the sounds that are most likely to be unfamiliar and that will probably cause thestudent the greatest difficulty.

If you've purchased this book as part of the *Complete Arabic: The Basics* package, you do not need to spend a great deal of time on Part 1, since the material is also covered in the coursebook. But if you're unfamiliar with the sounds of Arabic or the transcription system used in this book, you should start with Part 1. The audio is available online at www.livinglanguage.com if you do not have the recordings. You'll be able to improve your Arabic pronunciation by reading the descriptions of each sound and by practicing the examples. The transcription system used will be an easy introduction to the language, so you'll have a foundation to build on when you begin to learn written Arabic. Think of the transcription as "training wheels" that will make things easier for you when you move ahead.

PART 2: READING ARABIC

Once you're familiar with the sound system of Arabic, you'll be ready to see how those sounds are represented in written Arabic. Part 2 begins with an overview of the basics of written Arabic in plain and simple language. Then it presents the entire alphabet and introduces you to important concepts that are necessary to know before you tackle individual letters. The remainder of Part 2 presents Arabic letters in small, manageable groups. With each group, you'll learn the forms, and then you'll begin reading by practicing them in very simple syllables. Next, you'll see examples with simple words that only include the letters you've learned up to that point, so each group will build on the previous ones in a simple and straightforward progression. As you move ahead, you'll have plenty of chances to reinforce what you've already learned. There are a number of reading practice exercises that will allow you to learn how to read Arabic in short and easy steps. You'll be able to check your comprehension of the written Arabic by comparing it to the simple transcription provided. Every word or phrase used in the examples or practice exercises is also translated. Part 2 closes with additional practice exercises that include greetings and basic expressions, as well as simple sentences.

PART 3: WRITING ARABIC

Once you've learned how to read Arabic, writing it will be much easier. Part 3 follows the same simple, step-by-step progression used in Part 2. Letters are divided into small groups, and detailed explanations on how to write the different forms of the letters are provided, along with examples of written Arabic. You'll have the chance to practice the individual letters and simple syllables with them, and then you'll move on to words that include only the letters you've learned up to that point. Since you'll already have covered the material in the reading section, the transition in to writing Arabic will be much easier for you.

PART 4: READING PASSAGES

Finally, Part 4 will provide you with a chance to practice your reading skills with dialogues selected from *Complete Arabic: The Basics*. You'll have the chance to first read the fully voweled dialogues and then practice "real" written Arabic, which does not include short vowels or other symbols that are so useful to students of the language. The complete transcriptions and translations of each dialogue are also included.

Living Language offers a range of Arabic courses, allowing students to choose when (and if) they would like to tackle Arabic script. If you would prefer to focus on the spoken language first, we recommend *Complete Arabic: The Basics* or *Starting Out in Arabic*. If you would like to learn Arabic script from the beginning, we recommend *Ultimate Arabic*.

LIVING LANGUAGE COMPLETE ARABIC: THE BASICS

Complete Arabic: The Basics includes a coursebook with fifteen simple lessons and three hours of recordings. The recordings feature the pronunciation section that is included in this book, as well as dialogues recorded at two speeds, vocabulary lists, key grammar examples, and additional pronunciation practices. The coursebook also includes a grammar summary and a two-way learner's glossary. *Complete Arabic: The Basics* is a course in spoken Arabic. It does include sections on Arabic script with limited examples and practice, but since it is primarily a spoken language course, it uses, for the most part, a simple transcription system. This *Complete Guide to Arabic Script* is therefore perfect for students who are using *Complete Arabic: The Basics* and who would like to learn how to read and write Modern Standard Arabic after they've learned how to speak and understand it.

LIVING LANGUAGE STARTING OUT IN ARABIC

Starting Out in Arabic is an audio-only course in spoken Modern Standard Arabic. It is a simple, step-by-step introduction to the basics of Arabic. It features ten short lessons with basic vocabulary and grammar, as well as easy conversations and spoken practice. No book is necessary, so *Starting Out in Arabic* can be used anywhere. This program will give you a solid foundation in the basics of the spoken language, and if you choose to learn the script afterwards, you can move on to the *Complete Guide to Arabic Script* or one of the more comprehensive programs that include the written language.

LIVING LANGUAGE ULTIMATE ARABIC

Ultimate Arabic is a comprehensive course in Modern Standard Arabic, but it also includes an introduction to the spoken Egyptian, Iraqi, Lebanese, and Saudi varieties of Arabic. The course package includes a coursebook and eight hours of recordings, featuring dialogues, vocabulary, grammar, and culture notes. *Ultimate Arabic* teaches Arabic script, but *The Complete Guide to Arabic Script* can be used as a supplement for additional practice, so that students can master the written language. You may want to focus on the script before you begin the course, or you can supplement your *Ultimate Arabic* lessons with this book as you progress.

Part 1
Pronunciation and Transcription

Before we take a look at Arabic script, let's focus on the sounds of Arabic and how those sounds are represented in the transcription system used in this book. If you're already familiar with Arabic pronunciation and this transcription system, which is also presented in Lesson 1 of *Complete Arabic: The Basics,* you can skip ahead to Part 2, where you'll learn to read in Arabic.

Most of the sounds in Arabic are pronounced similarly to sounds in English, and in these cases the transcription system in this course simply uses the letters that represent those sounds. For example, there is a sound in Arabic that is pronounced just like the sound at the beginning of the English word *big,* so the transcription symbol used for that sound is *b.* There are other Arabic sounds that do not occur in English but are found in other European languages that you may be familiar with, such as French or German. But even if you're not familiar with these languages, the sounds are explained easily enough. Finally, there is a small number of sounds that may be very foreign to you, and these are probably the sounds that are most likely to give you trouble as a student of Arabic. But still, these sounds will be described in detail.

If you have the entire set of *Complete Arabic: The Basics,* you can listen to all of these sounds and practice pronouncing them. If you don't have the recordings, the descriptions of the sounds will give you a good idea of how to pronounce them, and you can find the audio at www.livinglanguage.com. Each example has been recorded by native speakers. That's because no matter how detailed a description of a sound is in one language, it can never completely capture that sound in another language, so the key to accurate pronunciation is to listen to native speakers, repeat, and practice.

Now we'll take a look at all of the sounds in Modern Standard Arabic and familiarize you with the transcription system used in this program. We'll divide the sounds into groups—vowels, the many sounds that may give you no trouble because they're very similar to sounds in English, the fewer sounds that will give you very little trouble because they're found in other languages you may be familiar with, and finally, the few difficult cases. You'll see the actual Arabic letter, its name, the transcription letter used in this course, a description of the sound, and several examples of Arabic words in which the sound occurs. Don't feel obligated to learn the actual Arabic letters just yet. This section is only meant to give you an overview of the sound system so that you'll be familiar with it when we tackle reading and writing. You'll have plenty of practice with the actual Arabic letters later.

VOWELS

There are three vowels in Modern Standard Arabic, but each one has both a long and a short variety. There are also two diphthongs, which are compound vowel sounds formed by gliding two sounds together. So, all in all, there are eight vowel sounds to focus on. Bear in mind that vowels in Arabic should always be clear and crisp, and they should never be reduced, as vowels often are in English.

كَتَبَ (write) = كُتُب (books)

/ a

The first short vowel in Arabic, called **fatHa,** is written as a short stroke on top of other letters. It can be pronounced like the *o* in *hot,* the *a* in *sat,* or like the *e* in *bet,* depending on the consonant before it. Consonants pronounced in the front of the mouth or with the teeth tend to make this sound more like *eh.*

wa (*and*)
man (*who*)
walad (*boy*)
kataba (*he wrote*)

/ u

The second short vowel in Arabic is **Damma.** It is written like a small, backwards *e* over another letter. It's pronounced like the vowel sound in *put* or *foot.*

kutub (*books*)
hum (*they*)
hunna (*they, f.*)
funduq (*hotel*)

/ i

The third and last short vowel in Arabic is **kasra,** written just like **fatHa,** but below the letter that carries it instead of above it. It's pronounced like the vowel in *sit* or *fit*.

bint (*girl*)

min (*from*)

'ism (*name*)

rijl (*foot*)

ا / aa

The long vowel **'alif,** which is also the first letter of the Arabic alphabet, is pronounced like the short *a*, but it's held longer. It can also sound like a long *eh*, depending on the consonant before it.

baab (*door*)
kitaab (*book*)
laa (*no*)
salaam (*peace*)

ya salam = really

و / uu

The long vowel written with the Arabic letter **waaw** is pronounced like the vowel in *pool* or *tool*. If you pronounce the English words *look* and *Luke,* but hold the vowel in *Luke*, you're pronouncing both the short *u* and the long *uu* of Arabic.

nuur (*light*)
duud (*worms*)
thuum (*garlic*)
katabuu (*they wrote*)

ي / ii

The long vowel written with the Arabic letter **yaa'** is pronounced like the vowel in *sea* or *me*. If you pronounce the English words *pit* and *Pete*, you're pronouncing the short Arabic *i* and the long Arabic *ii*.

diin (*religion*)
kabiir (*big*)   f = kabiira (ة)
qaSiir (*short*)   f = qasiira (ة)
'ismii (*my name*)

◦ و / aw

The compound sound, or diphthong, written with the letter **waaw** with a small circle over it is pronounced like the vowel in *house* or *brown*.

yawm (*day*)

khawkh (*peach, plum*)   خوخ

dhawq (*taste*)   thawq

xawm (*float*)

◦ ي / ay

The diphthong written with the letter **yaa'** with a small circle over it is pronounced like the vowel in *bait* or *late,* or sometimes like the vowel in *my* or *buy.*

bayt (*house*)

layla (*woman's name*)

kayf (*how*)

khayr (*goodness*)

CONSONANTS

Now let's take on the consonants. Remember that we'll use the convention of dividing them into three groups—the ones that are very similar to sounds found in English, the ones that occur in other familiar languages, and finally, the really tricky ones that generally give nonnative speakers of Arabic the hardest time.

Before we begin to look at the consonants, though, it's important to mention one point. There is a difference in pronunciation between single and double consonants in Arabic. A double consonant must be held longer than a single one. For example, the **n** in **'anaa** (*I*) is held for about half as long as the **nn** in **fannaan** (*artist*). This is easier to do with some consonants, such as **f, z, s, sh, th, n,** and **m,** which are produced with a continuous flow of air. Say these consonants aloud and you'll see that you can hold them for as long as your air supply lasts. Other consonants, such as **b, t, d,** or **k,** are produced by blocking airflow, so you can't hold them as you can the others. In these cases, pronounce the double consonants with a pause in the word. For example, **shubbaak** (*window*) sounds almost like two words—**shub** and then **baak.**

GROUP 1: SOUNDS THAT ARE SIMILAR TO ENGLISH

ب / b

The letter **baa'** is pronounced like the *b* in *boy* or *book*.

bint (*girl*) بِنْت

bayt (*house*) بَيْت

baab (*door*) باب

'al-baSra (*Basra*)

ت / t

The letter **taa'** is pronounced like the *t* in *take* or *tip*.

taktub (*you write*) تَكْتُب

tazuur (*you visit*)

tilmiidh (*pupil, student*)

fatHiyya (*woman's name*)

ö → ti → ة

(feminine)
ending

ث / th

The letter **thaa'** is pronounced like the *th* in *thank* or *think*. Be careful not to pronounce it like the *th* in *this* or *that*; this sound is a separate letter in Arabic.

thaaniya (*second*)

thalaatha (*three*)

thaa' (*the letter* th)

thuum (*garlic*)

[handwritten at top: jamil = M / jamila = F]

ج / j

The letter **jiim** is pronounced differently throughout the Arab world. In western and central North Africa as well as in the Levant, it is pronounced like the *zh* sound in *measure* or *pleasure*. In Egypt and Yemen, it is pronounced like the hard *g* in *go* or *get*. And in the eastern Arab world, it is pronounced like the *j* in *jelly* or *joke*.

jariida (*newspaper*) *[handwritten: my newspaper = jariidati]*

jamiil (*pretty*) *[handwritten: jamila = F also means "great"]*

jaziira (*island*) *[handwritten: = F]* *[handwritten: my island = jaziirati]*

jayyid (*good*)

[handwritten: F = jayyida جيّد]

د / d

The letter **daal** is pronounced like the *d* in *day* or *do*.

darasa (*he studied*) *[handwritten Arabic: درس]*

diin (*religion*)

dunyaa (*world*)

dimaagh (*brain*)

ذ / dh

The letter **dhaal** is pronounced like the *th* in *this*, *that*, or *other*. Do not confuse it with the *th* of *thank* or *think*.

dhahab (*gold*) *[handwritten Arabic: ذهب]*

dhahaba (*he went*) *[handwritten Arabic: ذهب]*

dhiraax (*arm*)

'ustaadh (*professor, m.*) F = ustaadha

ز / z

The letter **zaay** is pronounced like the *z* in *zoo* or *zipper*.

zaytuun (*olives*)

zaada (*he added*)

xaziiz (*man's name*) xaziiz = dear

zawj (*husband*) zawjati = my wife

my husband = zawji

س / s

The letter **siin** is pronounced like the *s* in *so* or *sit*.

samiik (*thick*)

rasm (*painting*) verb = rasama (past tense) = he drew

'islaam (*Islam*)

salaam (*peace, hello*)

ش / sh

The letter **shiin** is pronounced like the *sh* in *shoe* or *ship*.

shukran (*thank you*)

shams (*sun*) ش ـمـس

sharibat (*she drank*)

shaykh (*sheikh*)

ف / f

The letter **faa'** is pronounced like the *f* in *far* or *feel*.

fii (*in*)

faransaa (*France*)

fannaan (*artist*)   F = ڡ

fiil (*elephant*)

ك / k

The letter **kaaf** is pronounced like the *k* in *kite* or *keep*.

kitaab (*book*)

kalb (*dog*)

kayfa (*how*)

kursiyy (*chair*)

ل / l

The letter **laam** is pronounced like the *l* in *like* or *let*.

layl (*night*)

laa (*no*)

laTiif (*friendly*)

laysa (*he is not*)

م / m

The letter **miim** is pronounced like the *m* in *make* or *meet*.

maa (*what*)

masaa' (*evening*)

maktab (*office*)

mumtaaz (*wonderful, excellent*)

ن / n

The letter **nuun** is pronounced like the *n* in *now* or *neat*.

nuur (*light*)

'anaa (*I*)

nawm (*sleep*)

naxam (*yes*)

ه / h

The letter **haa'** is pronounced like the *h* in *here* or *happy*.

hunna (*they, f.*)

huduu' (*quiet*)

haadhaa (*this*)

hiya (*she*)

و / w

The letter **waaw** is pronounced like the *w* in *we* or *wool*. (It is also used in the Arabic alphabet to represent the long vowel in *tool* or *pool* and the diphthong in *house*.)

wa (*and*)

walad (*boy*)

waziir (*minister*)

waSala (*he arrived*) و صل

Saad.

ي / y

The letter **yaa'** is pronounced like the *y* in *yes* or *yellow*. (It is also used in the ˜Arabic alphabet to represent the long vowel in *week* or *see* and the diphthong in *bait*.)

yawm (*day*)

yaabaan (*Japan*)

yaktubu (*he writes*)

yasmiin (*jasmine*)

GROUP 2: SOUNDS THAT ARE SIMILAR TO OTHER EUROPEAN LANGUAGES

The following three consonants occur in other languages you may be familiar with.

خ / kh

The sound of the letter **khaa'** is not found in most varieties of English, but the sound at the end of the Scottish word *loch* is very close to it. It's also similar to the German sound in *Bach* or *Buch* or the Hebrew *baruch*. It's a deep, throaty sound like a tight, raspy *h*.

khawkh (*peach, plum*)

'akh (*brother*)

'ukht (*sister*)

khamsa (*five*)

ر / r

The sound of **raa'** is not the standard *r* of English, but rather, the rolled *r* of Italian or Spanish.

rajul (*man*)

rakhiiS (*inexpensive*)

rasm (*painting*)

ra's (*head*)

غ / gh

The sound of the letter **ghayn** is very similar to the *r* of the French words *rue* and *rare*. It comes from the back of the throat, near where *g* and *k* are produced. Imagine that you're about to gargle, and you'll pronounce **ghayn.**

ghadan (*tomorrow*)

ghariib (*strange*)

ghurfa (*room*)

dimaagh (*brain*)

GROUP 3: UNFAMILIAR SOUNDS

Finally, these are the sounds that are most likely to give you trouble, because they're unlike sounds in English or in other European languages.

ص / S

The letter **Saad** is pronounced like an emphatic, forceful *s*. It doesn't exist in English, but it's not difficult to make if you practice. Start by saying *s* as in *saw*, but then draw your tongue back and lower your jaw slightly. If you're having trouble doing this, just pronounce the long, deep *ahhhh* that you make when the doctor examines your throat. That will automatically put your tongue in the right position for **Saad**. **Saad, Daad, Taa',** and **DHaa'** change the quality of the vowels near them—they make them deeper. (Be careful in the transcription system to differentiate between **s,** which is like the English *s,* and **S.**)

aS-Siin (*China*)

Saghiir (*small*)

Sadiiq (*friend*)

SabaaH (*morning*)

ض / D

The letter **Daad** has the same relationship to the *d* in *day* as **Saad** has to the *s* in *say*. Practice in the same way—say a *d*, and then draw your tongue back and lower your jaw. Make the surrounding vowels deep.

Dabaab (*fog*)

Daruuriyy (*necessary*)

mariiD (*sick*)

Daxiif (*skinny*)

ط / T

The letter **Taa'** is a *t* with the tongue drawn back and the jaw lowered. Start with *t* as in *toy*, and make the same adjustments as you did for **S** and **D**.

Taqs (*weather*)

Tifl (*child*)

Taalib (*student*)

Taawila (*table*)

ظ / DH

The letter **DHaa'** is the last of the emphatic letters. It's the *th* in *this*, but pronounced with the tongue drawn back and the jaw lowered.

DHahr (*back*)

DHuhr (*noon*)

DHahara (*he appeared*)

DHalaam (*darkness*)

ق / q

The letter **qaaf** is similar to the sound of a *g* or a *k*, but it's produced further back in the throat, closer to where the sound of the gargled French *r* is produced. You should feel the constriction at the very back of your mouth, near the top of your throat.

qaa'id (*leader*)

qalb (*heart*)

qaamuus (*dictionary*)

Sadiiq (*friend*)

ء / '

The sound of the letter **hamza** isn't thought of as a "standard" English consonant, but if you know what to listen for, you'll hear that it's far from rare. In fact, you produce it every time you say *uh-oh!* It's technically called a glottal stop, because it's a quick block in the airflow through your mouth caused by closing the very top of your throat, the glottis. But you don't need to get so technical to make this sound. Think of the Cockney pronunciation of the words *bottle* and *settle,* with a short, gentle coughing sound where the double *t* is written. There are also many regional American accents that use a very similar sound to pronounce the final *t* in words like *put, cat,* and *sit.* Notice that this sound is transcribed with an apostrophe, but remember that it's a full, bona fide consonant in Arabic. In fact, it occurs in the names of many of the Arabic letters. Make sure you pronounce it when you see it.

ka's (*glass*)

maa' (*water*)

qara'a (*he read*)

maa'ida (*board*)

You'll also see this letter at the beginning of Arabic words that start with a vowel. Don't make any special effort to pronounce the **hamza** at the beginning of words. It's natural, even in English, to automatically produce a glottal stop whenever you begin to pronounce a word that starts with a vowel. The **hamza** is included in the transcription in these cases because, as you'll see, all Arabic words that begin with a vowel sound are written with **hamza.**

'ayna (*where*)

'adrusu (*I study*)

'awlaad (*boys*)

'ibn (*son*)

ح / H

The sound of the letter **Haa'** is perhaps the second hardest Arabic sound to make. But again, you've probably made this sound many times. Imagine that you're lowering yourself into a very hot bath. That very forceful *Ha!*–with some constriction at the top of your throat is the sound of **Haa'.** You might also make this sound when you've put too much jalapeño in your chili or too much wasabi on your sushi. Or you might make this sound when you blow on your glasses to clean them. The only difficulty in pronouncing **Haa'** probably comes from the fact that you think of it as an exclamation rather than as a consonant. If you get used to that, you'll have no trouble pronouncing **Haa'**.

Haarr (*hot*)

Hajar (*stone*)

masraH (*theater*)

miSbaaH (*lamp*)

ع / x

Following the tradition of leaving the best for last, the letter **xayn** is almost definitely the hardest Arabic sound to pronounce. It's similar to the very emphatic **H** of **Haa'**, but it vibrates as well, and airflow is just about choked off by constriction at the top of the throat. You use the necessary muscles when you gag, and if you put your fingers on your throat and make yourself gag slightly, you'll feel the muscles you'll need to produce **xayn**. Again, it's not that it's impossible to produce this sound, but it's hard to get used to the idea that it's a regular consonant in a language. In Arabic, it's even a common consonant!

al-xarabiyya (*Arabic language*)

xalaykum (*on you*)

'al-xiraaq (*Iraq*)

faxaltu (*I did*)

Now that you're familiar with the overall sound system in Arabic, let's move on to reading Arabic.

Part 2
Reading Arabic

THE BASICS

The most basic thing to know about Arabic script is that it's written and read from right to left. That means that Arabic books have their spines on the right and open from the left. Another basic fact about written Arabic is that only long vowels are usually written. As you know, Arabic has two types of vowels–long, which we've transcribed as **aa, ii,** and **uu,** and short, which we've transcribed as **a, i,** and **u.** The short vowels are usually not written in "real" Arabic. Arabic also has diphthongs (**aw, ay**), but only the letters **w** and **y** are typically written. Just as a point of comparison, this means that if English were written like Arabic, the word *son* would be written *sn,* but *soon* would be spelled out. Short vowels do appear sometimes–in the Koran, in children's books, and in language courses like this one. They take the form of strokes or swirls above or below the conso- nant they're pronounced after. So *son* might look something like S°N, or rather, N°S in the order in which Arabic words are written.

THE ARABIC ALPHABET

There are twenty-eight letters in the Arabic alphabet. Arabic is a cursive script, meaning that most letters are connected to the ones before and after them. There are a few letters that don't connect to the ones that come after them, but we'll cover those later.

Because Arabic letters (usually) connect to whatever comes before or after them, each letter has a different shape depending on where it's written:

- Independent: This is the form that's used when a letter is written separately, in isolation from any other letter.

- Initial: This is the form that's used when a letter begins a word or comes after a non-connecting letter. It usually only has a connecting stroke on the left side.

- Medial: This is the form that's used when a letter comes in between two other (connecting) letters. It has a connecting stroke on either side, or just on the right side if it is non-connecting.

- Final: This is the form that's used when a letter comes at the end of a word. It only has a connecting stroke on the right.

Let's look at an example. Here are the four forms of **baa'**, which is pronounced like the first sound in *Baghdad*. Notice where the connecting tail is on the initial, medial, and final forms, and that there is no connecting stroke on the independent form.

LETTER	SOUND	FINAL	MEDIAL	INITIAL	INDEPENDENT
baa'	b	ـب	ـبـ	بـ	ب

Now take a look at an example of a non-connecting letter, **daal**, as in *Dubai*. Logically, because it doesn't connect to letters that come after it, its independent and initial forms are identical, as are its medial and final forms.

verb= 3 consonants

LETTER	SOUND	FINAL	MEDIAL	INITIAL	INDEPENDENT
daal	**d**	ـد	ـد	د	د

Now let's take a look at the entire Arabic alphabet. You'll notice that only the long vowels ا **aa**, و **uu**, and ي **ii** appear on the chart, and that و and ي are also the consonants **w** and **y** respectively. Also note that Arabic letters are grouped by shape. For example, the letters ب, ت, and ث (pronounced **b, t,** and **th**) only differ in the number and location of dots, so they appear together in the alphabet.

Don't worry about memorizing each letter at this point. This section is only meant to give you an overview of the Arabic alphabet. In the sections that follow, we'll divide the letters into small, manageable groups, so you'll have plenty of step-by-step practice both in reading and in writing.

جرح =heran =jara

LETTER	SOUND	FINAL	MEDIAL	INITIAL	INDEPENDENT
alif	**a , aa**	ـا	ـا	ا	ا
baa'	**b**	ـب	ـبـ	بـ	ب
taa'	**t**	ـت	ـتـ	تـ	ت
thaa'	**th**	ـث	ـثـ	ثـ	ث
jiim	**j**	ـج	ـجـ	جـ	ج
Haa'	**H**	ـح	ـحـ	حـ	ح
khaa'	**kh**	ـخ	ـخـ	خـ	خ

جرح =scratch

جرحي =my scratch =jarhi

brother = أخ

sister = oukhti

he left = خرج

house= رار

جبل = rock
جبال = rooms
جبلة = room

درس = he studied

daal	d	ـد	ـد	د	د
dhaal	dh	ـذ	ـذ	ذ	ذ
raa'	r	ـر	ـر	ر	ر
zaay	z	ـز	ـز	ز	ز
siin	s	ـس	ـسـ	ـس	س
shiin	sh	ـش	ـشـ	ـش	ش
Saad	S	ـص	ـصـ	ـص	ص
Daad	D	ـض	ـضـ	ـض	ض
Taa'	T	ـط	ـطـ	ـط	ط
DHaa'	DH	ـظ	ـظـ	ـظ	ظ
xayn	x	ـع	ـعـ	عـ	ع

secret = سر

my secret = سري

شجر = tree

شجرة = f. tree = 1 tree

oorz = أرز = rice

ti = S

ghayn	gh	غ‍	‍غ‍	‍غ‍	غ
faa'	f	‍ف	‍ف‍	ف‍	ف
qaaf	q	‍ق	‍ق‍	ق‍	ق
kaaf	k	‍ك	‍كـ	كـ	ك
laam	l	‍ل	‍لـ	لـ	ل
miim	m	‍م	‍مـ	مـ	م
nuun	n	‍ن	‍نـ	نـ	ن
haa'	h	‍ه	‍هـ	هـ	ة*
waaw	w, uu	‍و	‍و	و	و
yaa'	y, ii	‍ي	‍يـ	يـ	ي

*femine ending

To review the pronunciation of any of these letters, refer to Part 1.

CONNECTING AND NON-CONNECTING LETTERS

Notice that among the three long vowels, ي is a connecting letter, and ١ and و are not. Don't forget that و and ي are also the consonants **w** and **y** respectively. There are only four other non-connecting letters, all of which are consonants: د **d**, ذ **dh**, ر **r**, and ز **z**.

READING PRACTICE 1

Scan the following words and see if you can identify the non-connecting letters, setting aside the final ones for now. Don't worry if you can't read the words yet. We'll divide the alphabet into small groups and tackle each letter step-by-step in a moment.

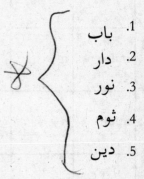

1. باب
2. دار
3. نور
4. ثوم
5. دين

Answers

1. **baab** (*door*, non-connecting letter is ١), 2. **daar** (*house*, non-connecting letters are د and ١), 3. **nuur** (*light*, non-connecting letter is و), 4. **thuum** (*garlic*, non-connecting letter is و), 5. **diin** (*religion*, non-connecting letter is د)

Now let's take a look at individual groups of letters, so you can practice reading Arabic step-by-step.

GROUP 1: LONG VOWELS

Let's start with long vowels. **'alif** and **waaw** are non-connecting letters, so they only have two forms. When **'alif** is at the beginning of a word, it has a small **hamza**, like a backwards 2, written above or below it, but we'll explain that later. For now just be aware of it. **yaa'** is a connecting letter, so it has four forms. The letters و and ي also represent the consonants **w** and **y** respectively.

LETTER	SOUND	FINAL	MEDIAL	INITIAL	INDEPENDENT
'alif	a, aa	ﻝ	ﻞ	ا / أ	ا / أ
waaw	w, uu	ﻮ	ﻮ	و	و
yaa'	y, ii	ﻲ	ﻴ	ﻳ	ى

GROUP 2: SHORT VOWELS AND DIPHTHONGS

Now let's add the short vowels. The vowel **fatHa** is written as a slash above the consonant that "hosts" it: ´, **Damma** is like a small hook: ُ, and **kasra** is a slash below the consonant: ِ. Let's see how that works, using the consonants و and ي to host these short vowels.

´ (a)	وَ (wa)	يَ (ya)
ُ (u)	وُ (wu)	يُ (yu)
ِ (i)	وِ (wi)	يِ (yi)

READING PRACTICE 2

Practice reading these syllables, which use the consonants و and ي, as well as both long and short vowels.

1. وَ	3. يَ	5. وُ	7. يُ
2. يا	4. يو	6. وِ	8. يِي

Answers

1. **wa**, 2. **yaa**, 3. **ya**, 4. **yuu**, 5. **wu**, 6. **wi**, 7. **yu**, 8. **yii**

Now let's look at the diphthongs **aw** and **ay**. These are written with **fatHa** over the (preceding) host consonant, and then a special symbol called **sukuun,** which is a small open circle: وْ (**aw**), يْ (**ay**). The role of the **sukuun** (which means *silent* or *quiet*) is to indicate that there's no vowel pronounced after و and ي—in other words, they're part of the **fatHa** before them. This gives the combination sound of the diphthong: **aw** or **ay**.

وَيْ (**way**)	يَوْ (**yaw**)

READING PRACTICE 3

Practice pronouncing these example syllables, sounding each one out step-by-step.

1. يَوْ	3. وَيْ
2. يَىْ	4. وَوْ

1. **yaw,** 2. **yay,** 3. **way,** 4. **waw**

GROUP 3: ب b, ت t, AND ث th

Now let's look at our first group of consonants. The consonants ب, ت, and ث differ from one another only in the number and placement of dots. They're pronounced **b, t,** and **th** respectively. Keep in mind that ث is pronounced like the *th* in *think,* not like the *th* in *this,* which is a different letter in Arabic.

LETTER	SOUND	FINAL	MEDIAL	INITIAL	INDEPENDENT
baa'	b	ـب	ـبـ	بـ	ب
taa'	t	ـت	ـتـ	تـ	ت
thaa'	th	ـث	ـثـ	ثـ	ث

With long vowels, short vowels, diphthongs, and a few consonants under your belt, you're ready to tackle your first Arabic words.

door	**baab**	بَاب
houses	**buyuut**	بُيُوتْ
he stood firm	**thabata**	ثَبَتَ

Before we look at other consonants, let's see how words that begin with short vowels are written. In these cases, the first letter is **'alif,** but it's only used to "carry" the short vowel, so it's not pronounced on its own. **'alif** is written with a small **hamza,** like a backwards number 2, and the short vowel. **hamza** is written above **'alif** if the vowel is **fatHa** or **Damma,** but below **'alif** if the vowel is **kasra.** In fully voweled Arabic, which, again, is not typical, you'll have both a **hamza** and the short vowel along with **'alif.** So, أَ is pronounced **'a,** أُ is pronounced **'u,** and إِ is pronounced **'i.**

أَب ('**ab**)	إِث ('**ith**)	أَث ('**ath**)
إِب ('**ib**)	أُت ('**ut**)	إِت ('**it**)

READING PRACTICE 4

Practice reading each of the following words, which include the vowels and consonants you've learned. Take your time with each one, and sound out each consonant and vowel step-by-step.

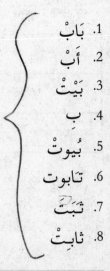

1. بَابْ
2. أَبْ
3. بَيْتْ
4. بِ
5. بُيوتْ
6. تَابوت
7. ثَبَّتَ
8. ثابِتْ

Answers

1. **baab** (*door*), 2. **'ab** (*father*), 3. **bayt** (*house*), 4. **bi** (*in, at, on, with*),
5. **buyuut** (*houses*), 6. **taabuut** (*coffin, casket*), 7. **thabata** (*he stood firm*),
8. **thaabit** (*fixed, firm*)

thabita (she stood firm)

GROUP 4: ج j, ح h, and خ kh

The consonants ج, ح, and خ are another trio that differ only in the placement (or presence) of a dot. Notice that only the independent and final forms have tails.

LETTER	SOUND	FINAL	MEDIAL	INITIAL	INDEPENDENT
jiim	j	ج	ج	ج	ج
Haa'	H	ح	ح	ح	ح
Khaa'	kh	خ	خ	خ	خ

Here are some example words.

sister	**'ukht**	أُخْت
obligation, necessity	**wujuub**	وُجُوب
argument, debate	**Hijaaj**	حَجَاج "ee"
jeep	**jiib***	جيب

*Notice that because there's no *p* in Arabic, loanwords with *p* are written with ب.

READING PRACTICE 5

Now practice reading these words, which use the letters that you've learned so far.

1. جِباب

2. جَبْح

3. حَبِيب

4. حُبَاحِبْ

5. حَيْثُ

6. خَبَبْ

7. خَبُثَ

8. خَبِيثٌ

[handwritten notes in margin: "F-habibti M-habibi", "habibti", "حبيبي"]

Answers

1. **jibaab** (*jubbahs*, a type of garment), 2. **jabH** (*beehive*), 3. **Habiib** (*sweetie, love*), 4. **HubaaHib** (*fireflies*), 5. **Haythu** (*where, since*), 6. **khabab** (*trot*), 7. **khabutha** (*to be bad, wicked*), 8. **khabiith** (*evil, wicked*)

[handwritten note: "cunning"]

GROUP 5: د d, ذ dh, م m AND ز z

Now let's add four more consonants. The pairs د / ذ and ر / ز obviously differ in the presence of a dot, but they're also all similar in that they're non-connecting letters, so they only have two forms each. Note that د and ذ sit on top of the line, while ر and ز

extend below it. The letter ذ is *th* as in *this* or *the*, not *th* as in *think* or *three*, which is, of course, written ث.

LETTER	SOUND	FINAL	MEDIAL	INITIAL	INDEPENDENT
daal	d	ـد	ـدـ	د	د
dhaal	dh	ـذ	ـذـ	ذ	ذ
raa'	r	ـر	ـرـ	ر	ر
zaay	z	ـز	ـزـ	ز	ز

sea	baHr	بَحْر
radar	raadaar	رادار
he drove back	zajara *(raja-ah)*	زَجَرَ
sharp	dharib	ذَرِبْ

READING PRACTICE 6

Practice reading these words.

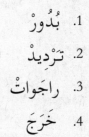

1. بُدُورْ
2. تَرْدِيدْ
3. راجَواتْ
4. خَرَجَ

5. خَدِرْ

6. حَرِجْ

7. إِحْتِرابْ

8. ذَبْذَبَ

9. ذَواتْ

10. رَوْد

11. زُيُوتْ

12. زَوَر

13. زَواجْ

14. زِيرْ

Answers

1. **buduur** (*full moons*), 2. **tardiid** (*repetition*), 3. **raajawaat** (*rajas, Indian princes*), 4. **kharaja** (*he left*), 5. **khadir** (*numb*), 6. **Harij** (*confined*), 7. **'iHtiraab** (*struggle*), 8. **dhabdhaba** (*he swung, dangled*), 9. **dhawaat** (*essences, natures*), 10. **rawd** (*exploration*), 11. **zuyuut** (*oils*), 12. **zawar** (*slant*), 13. **zawaaj** (*marriage*), 14. **ziir** (*large water jars*)

GROUP 6: س s AND ش sh

Now let's add two more similar-looking consonants, س and ش, which are pronounced **s** and **sh**. Once again, only the independent and final forms have tails.

LETTER	SOUND	FINAL	MEDIAL	INITIAL	INDEPENDENT
siin	s	ـس	ـسـ	سـ	س
shiin	sh	ـش	ـشـ	شـ	ش

sixth	saadis	سَادِس
political	siyaasiyy	سِياسِي
gray hair, old age	shayb	شَيْب
sheikh, chief	shaykh	شَيْخ

READING PRACTICE 7

Here are some more words to practice with the letters we've covered so far.

1. سُوريا
2. سَبَحَتْ
3. شَاي
4. شَرِبْتُ
5. أَسْوَد
6. دَرَسْتُ
7. تَشَاوَرَ

8. أَشْجَر

9. سَادَاتْ

10. سُوسْ

Answers

1. **suuriyaa** (*Syria*), 2. **sabaHat** (*she swam*), 3. **shaay** (*tea*), 4. **sharibtu** (*I drank*), 5. **'aswad** (*black*), 6. **darastu** (*I studied*), 7. **tashaawara** (*he consulted*), 8. **'ashjar** (*wooded*), 9. **saadaat** (*master, sir, honorable*), 10. **suus** (*licorice*)

GROUP 7: ص S, ض D, ط T, AND ظ DH

Now let's look at the "emphatic" consonants **S**, **D**, **T**, and **DH**. These consonants give the vowels around them a very deep quality, coming from the throat. Lower your jaw to increase the size of the space in which the surrounding vowels are pronounced. Notice that these letters all have a "hump" and that they come in two pairs that differ only in the presence of a dot.

LETTER	SOUND	FINAL	MEDIAL	INITIAL	INDEPENDENT
Saad	S	ـص	ـصـ	صـ	ص
Daad	D	ـض	ـضـ	ضـ	ض
Taa'	T	ـط	ـطـ	طـ	ط
DHaa'	DH	ـظ	ـظـ	ظـ	ظ

owner	SaaHib	صَاحِب
he grabbed	DabaTa	ضَبَطَ
doctor	Tabiib	طَبِيب
lucky	HaDHiiDH	حَظِيظ

READING PRACTICE 8

Here are some words to practice reading.

1. صَبَاح

2. صَحِيح

3. ضَجِرَت

4. إِضْرَار

5. طَبْخ

6. بَطَاطِس

7. حِظَار

8. حَاضِر

9. تَخَاطُب

10. وَسَط

Answers

1. **SabaaH** (*morning*), 2. **SaHiiH** (*true*), 3. **Dajirat** (*she was angry*),
4. **'iDraar** (*harm, injury*), 5. **Tabkh** (*cooking*), 6. **baTaaTis** (*potatoes*),
7. **HiDHaar** (*partition, screen*), 8. **HaaDir** (*present, in attendance*),
9. **takhaaTub** (*discussion*), 10. **wasaT** (*middle*)

GROUP 8: ع x AND غ gh

The pair ع and غ are again only different in the placement of a dot over غ. But notice that both of these letters have forms that look quite different depending on where they are in a word, and only the final and independent forms have tails.

LETTER	SOUND	FINAL	MEDIAL	INITIAL	INDEPENDENT
xayn	x	ع	ـعـ	عـ	ع
ghayn	gh	ـغ	ـغـ	غـ	غ

Arabic	xarabiyy	عَرَبِي
not	ghayr	غَيْر
small	Saghiir	صَغِير
Baghdad	baghdaad	بَغْدَاد

READING PRACTICE 9

Here are some more words to practice the letters that you've learned so far.

1. عَرُوس
2. أَعزَب
3. رَبِيع
4. صِرَاع
5. تَاسِع
6. غَرْبِي
7. دَغْدَغ
8. غُبَار

Answers

1. **xaruus** (*bride*), 2. **'axzab** (*single*), 3. **rabiix** (*spring*), 4. **Siraax** (*struggle*), 5. **taasix** (*ninth*), 6. **gharbiyy** (*western*), 7. **daghdagha** (*he tickled*), 8. **ghubaar** (*dust*)

GROUP 9: ف f AND ق q

The pair ف f and ق q differ in the number of dots they have and also where they are positioned relative to the line. Notice that ق crosses below the line, while ف remains on it.

LETTER	SOUND	FINAL	MEDIAL	INITIAL	INDEPENDENT
faa'	f	ـف	ـفـ	فـ	ف
qaaf	q	ـق	ـقـ	قـ	ق

in	fii	فِي
guest	Dayf	ضَيْف
short	qaSiir	قَصِير
contracts	xuquud	عُقود

READING PRACTICE 10

And now practice reading words that include ف, ق, and other letters that you know.

1. دَفَعْتُ

2. صَدِيق

3. صَحَفِي

4. شُقَق

5. سُوق

6. يَقُود

7. قَفْز

8. فَقَط

Answers

1. **dafaxtu** (*I paid*), 2. **Sadiiq** (*friend*), 3. **SaHafiyy** (*journalist*),
4. **shuqaq** (*apartments*), 5. **suuq** (*market*), 6. **yaquud** (*he leads*), 7. **qafz**
(*jumping*), 8. **faqaT** (*only*)

GROUP 10: ك k, ل l, م m, AND ن n

Now let's add four more consonants to the list: **k, l, m,** and **n**. With
these four, you're just about done! Notice that the independent and
final forms of ك have a small *s*-like stroke, but the medial and initial
forms don't. And notice that the independent and final forms of ل
have a hook that falls beneath the lines, but the medial and initial
forms don't. م and ن also fall below the line in their independent and
final forms. In its medial and initial forms, ن looks similar to ب, but the
dot is above rather than below the letter.

LETTER	SOUND	FINAL	MEDIAL	INITIAL	INDEPENDENT
kaaf	k	ـك	ـكـ	كـ	ك
laam	l	ـل	ـلـ	لـ	ل
miim	m	ـم	ـمـ	مـ	م
nuun	n	ـن	ـنـ	نـ	ن

meat	laHm	لَحْم
nights	layaalii	لَيَالِي
chair	kursii	كُرْسِي
yes	naxam	نَعَم
resident	saakin	سَاكِن
your name	'ismuka	إسْمُكَ

READING PRACTICE 11

Here are several more words to practice.

1. مَشْرِق

2. كَثِير

3. مُدُن

4. قَلَم

5. مِسْمَار

6. لَكِن

7. أَنا

8. عِلْم

9. أَكَلْتُ

10. مَطَار

11. رِيَال

12. جَمِيل

Answers

1. **mashriq** (*east*), 2. **kathiir** (*many*), 3. **mudun** (*cities*), 4. **qalam** (*pen*),
5. **mismaar** (*nail*), 6. **lakin** (*but*), 7. **'anaa** (*I*), 8. **xilm** (*knowledge*),
9. **'akaltu** (*I ate*), 10. **maTaar** (*airport*), 11. **riyaal** (*riyal*), 12. **jamiil** (*beautiful*)

GROUP 11: ه h AND ة taa' marbuuTa

Now let's look at ه, or **h**, which is the last consonant that you need to learn, as well as ة, or final **a**, which looks very similar but is actually a short **a** in final position. ة is a very typical feminine ending in Arabic, pronounced exactly the same as **fatHa**. It's called **taa' marbuuTa**, or "tied **t**," because it has a hidden **t** sound that is sometimes pronounced. Notice that it has no medial or initial forms, because it only occurs at the end of words. The independent form is used when it follows a non-connecting letter.

LETTER	SOUND	FINAL	MEDIAL	INITIAL	INDEPENDENT
haa'	h	ـه	ـهـ	هـ	ه
taa' marbuuTa	a	ـة			ة

river	nahr	نَهْر
she went	dhahabat	ذَهَبَت
he	huwa	هُوَ
cow	baqara	بَقَرَة
princess	'amiira	أَمِيرَة

READING PRACTICE 12

Now practice reading words with these letters.

1. هِيَ

2. هَذِهِ

3. هُنَاك

4. ظَهْر

5. جَامِعة

6. غُرْفة

7. كُرة

8. فَهِمْت

9. أَذْهَب

10. مَدِينة

11. زَهْرة

12. عَهْد

Answers

1. **hiya** (*she*), 2. **haadhihi** (*this* [*f.*]), 3. **hunaak** (*there*), 4. **DHahr** (*back*),
5. **jaamixa** (*university*), 6. **ghurfa** (*room*), 7. **kura** (*ball*), 8. **fahimt**
(*I understood*), 9. **'adhhab** (*I go*), 10. **madiina** (*city*), 11. **zahra** (*blossom*),
12. **xahd** (*era*)

READING PRACTICE 13

Practice reading the following words, which mix all of the consonants you've learned so far with short and long vowels.

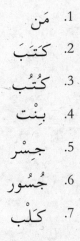

1. مَن

2. كَتَبَ

3. كُتُب

4. بِنْت

5. جِسْر

6. جُسُور

7. كَلْب

8. فِي

9. رِجَال

10. نَعَم

11. فُنْدُق

12. وَلَد

Answers

1. **man** (*who*), 2. **kataba** (*he wrote*), 3. **kutub** (*books*), 4. **bint** (*girl*),
5. **jisr** (*bridge*), 6. **jusuur** (*bridges*), 7. **kalb** (*dog*), 8. **fii** (*in*), 9. **rijaal** (*men*),
10. **naxam** (*yes*), 11. **funduq** (*hotel*), 12. **walad** (*boy*)

READING PRACTICE 14

Practice reading the following words as a general review.

1. حَبِيب

2. بِجَانِبِ

3. شَمْس

4. صَوْت

5. تِلْمِيذ

6. شَيْخ

7. نَوْم

8. قَلْب

9. صَدِيق

10. ظُهْر

11. بِنْت

12. مَطْعَم

13. مِصْر

14. يَوْم

15. ذَوْق

Answers

1. **Habiib** (*beloved*), 2. **bijaanibi** (*next to*), 3. **shams** (*sun*), 4. **Sawt** (*sound*),
5. **tilmiidh** (*student, pupil*), 6. **shaykh** (*sheikh*), 7. **nawm** (*sleep*), 8. **qalb**
(*heart*), 9. **Sadiiq** (*friend*), 10. **DHuhr** (*noon*), 11. **bint** (*girl*), 12. **maTxam**
(*restaurant*), 13. **miSr** (*Egypt*), 14. **yawm** (*day*), 15. **dhawq** (*taste*)

Now you've learned all of the consonants, the long vowels, the short
vowels and **taa' marbuuTa**, and the diphthongs and **sukuun**.
You've also seen how **hamza** is used with **'alif** in words that begin
with short vowels. There are just a few more symbols and special letters to know. We'll also spend some more time with **hamza**, because
its use in spelling is difficult to master.

GROUP 12: shadda, laam-'alif, AND THE DEFINITE ARTICLE
The small symbol **shadda**, which looks like a 3 on its side, is placed
above consonants to show that they're doubled. You should hold the
consonant sound for twice as long when you see **shadda**
(or when you know it should be there, because it's not always written!). Remember that **kasra** is usually written below the consonant
that it's pronounced after, but it can also be written below **shadda** on
top of the hosting consonant. The vowel **fatHa** is written above
shadda.

every	kull	كُلّ
meter, counter	xaddaad	عَدَّاد
bathroom	Hammaam	حَمَّام
teacher	mudarris	مُدَرِّس

The special combination letter **لا laam-'alif** is used for the pronunciation **laa**–in other words, when ا follows ل. It's used to avoid too many similar looking vertical strokes in a row. And speaking of **laam** and **'alif**, that same combination in the other order gives you the definite article أل. (For some reason, the two vertical strokes in a row don't matter in this order!) In writing and in speech, the article is attached to the words that follow it.

no	laa	لا
Venezuela	finizwiilaa	فِنِزْويلا
necessary	laazim	لازِم
the book	'al-kitaab	ألكِتاب
the boy	'al-walad	ألوَلَد

Don't forget that ل is sometimes pronounced like the consonant that follows it, in the case of "sun" letters. The sun letters are: ت t, ث th, د d, ذ dh, ر r, ز z, س s, ش sh, ص S, ض D, ط T, ظ DH, and ن n. Notice that they're all pronounced with the tongue near the teeth. The definite article is always written أل, but in pronunciation, the ل is pronounced like a sun letter if the article comes before it.

the reason	'as-sabab	ألسَّبَب
the table	'aT-Taawila	ألطَّاوِلة
the sun	'ash-shams	ألشَّمْس
the man	'ar-rajul	ألرَّجُل

And remember that if a word starts with a short vowel, it will be spelled with an **'alif**, which may include **hamza** and **fatHa** if the text is fully voweled. That means that if there's a definite article in front of such a word, the combination will be أ + ل + أ. In spelling, this will be **'alif**, followed by **laam-'alif**.

| the name | 'al-'ism | ألإِسْم |
| the family | 'al-'usra | ألأُسْرة |

READING PRACTICE 15

Now let's practice reading this group.

1. سِتَّة

2. مَمَرّ

3. حَمَّام

4. كُلّ

5. لاحِق

6. سَلام

7. طُلاب

8. أَلْبَيْت

9. أَلرَجُل

10. أَلْيَوْم

11. أَلأُخْت

12. أَلأَوْلاد

Answers

1. **sitta** (*six*), 2. **mamarr** (*corridor*), 3. **Hammaam** (*bathroom*), 4. **kull** (*each*), 5. **laaHiq** (*later*), 6. **salaam** (*peace*), 7. **Tulaab** (*students*), 8. **'al-bayt** (*the house*), 9. **'ar-rajul** (*the man*), 10. **'al-yawm** (*the day*), 11. **'al-'ukht** (*the sister*), 12. **'al-'awlaad** (*the boys*)

13: hamza

You already know that words that begin with a short vowel are written in Arabic with a **hamza**. The **hamza** is written like a small backwards 2, and it sits on top of or below an **'alif**. The **'alif** itself isn't pronounced; it's just a host for the **hamza** and the short vowel. So, أ is pronounced **'a**, أ is pronounced **'u**, and إ is pronounced **'i**.

READING PRACTICE 16

Here are a few more words to practice, all of which begin with short vowels.

١. أَنا

٢. إِبْن

٣. أُخْت

٤. أَرْبَعة

٥. أُسْتاذة

٦. إجازة

٧. أَمْريكي

٨. إِمْتِحان

Answers

1. **'anaa** (*I*), 2. **'ibn** (*son*), 3. **'ukht** (*sister*), 4. **'arbaxa** (*four*), 5. **'ustaadha** (*professor, f.*), 6. **'ijaaza** (*vacation*), 7. **'amriikii** (*American*), 8 **'imtiHaan** (*exam*)

hamza can also occur in the middle of a word or at the end, in which cases it may be written above **'alif, waaw,** or (dotless) **yaa'** as أ, ؤ, or ئ or it can even stand on its own as ء. The Arabic spelling rules for **hamza** are rather complicated, and it's much easier to recognize **hamza** in a word than to know how to write a word with **hamza** if you're unfamiliar with it. As much as possible, you should try to memorize how **hamza** is written in different environments, and eventually you'll get a feel for it. But here are some generalizations that can help you.

We'll start with **hamza** in the middle of a word. If the vowel after **hamza** is **fatHa**, word-internal **hamza** is written as أ. If there is a **sukuun** after **hamza** and the vowel before it is **fatHa**, it's also written as أ.

woman	'imraa'a	إِمْرَأَة
he asked	sa'ala	سَأَلَ
head	ra's	رَأْس
mouse (f.)	fa'ra	فَأْرة

If the vowel following **hamza** is **Damma**, word-internal **hamza** is written as ؤ. If there's a **sukun** or a **Damma** after **hamza** and the vowel before it is **Damma**, it's also written as ؤ.

curious, nosy, prying	sa'uul	سَؤُول
request, demand	su'l	سُؤْل
management	tara'us	تَرَؤُّس
sight	ru'ya	رُؤْية

If the vowel following or preceding **hamza** is **kasra**, word-internal **hamza** is written as ئـ. If there's a long ي before **hamza**, or if the diphthong **'ay** follows **hamza**, it's also written as ئـ. Notice that in this use, ئـ loses its two dots.

family	xaa'ila	عَائِلة
specialist	'akhaSSa'ii	أَخَصَّئي
Algeria	al-jazaa'ir	ألجَزائِر
main	ra'iisii	رَئيسي
airplane	Taa'ira	طَائِرة

Word-internal **hamza** can also be written on its own, as ء, if the vowel after it is **fatHa**.

reading	qiraa'a	قِراءة

At the end of a word, **hamza** may be written on its own. In some cases, especially in verbs, it can also be written above an **'alif**.

evening	masaa'	مَساء
women	nisaa'	نِساء
he was wholesome	hana'a	هَنَأَ

READING PRACTICE 17

Practice reading the following words with **hamza** in different positions.

1. أهلا وَ سَهلاً
2. إسْمُكِ
3. أشْيَاء
4. مِن أيْن
5. أحْيَاء
6. أنْتَ
7. أسْكُن
8. أمْريكِيّة
9. الأرْبِعاء

10. قَرَأَ

11. يَقْرَأْ

12. أَبُو ظَبْي

13. أَبْيَض

14. إِمَام

15. دَقَائِق

16. إِيجَار

17. أَسْمَاء

18. أُذُن

Answers

1. **'ahlan wa sahlan** (*hello*), 2. **'ismuki** (*your name* [*f.*]), 3. **'ashyaa'** (*things*), 4. **min 'ayn** (*where from*), 5. **'aHyaa'** (*biology*), 6. **'anta** (*you*), 7. **'askun** (*I live*), 8. **'amriikiyya** (*American* [*f.*]), 9. **al-'arbixaa'** (*Wednesday*), 10. **qara'a** (*he read*), 11. **yaqra'** (*he reads*), 12. **'abuu Dhabyi** (*Abu Dhabi*), 13. **'abyaD** (*white*), 14. **'imaam** (*imam*), 15. **daqaa'iq** (*minutes*), 16. **'iijaar** (*rent*), 17. **'asmaa'** (*names*), 18. **'udhun** (*ear*)

14: 'alif maqSuura

'alif maqSuura looks just like ي, but without the dots: ى. It's pronounced like a long **aa**, and it often replaces ا. It only occurs at the end of words, although non-Arabic borrowings typically retain ا instead of ى.

to	'ilaa	إلى
to tell	Hakaa	حَكَى

READING PRACTICE 18

Practice reading the following words with **'alif maqSuura**.

١. عَلى

٢. يَبْقى

٣. حَتَّى

٤. لَيْلى

Answers

1. **xalaa** (*on*), 2. **yabqaa** (*stays*), 3. **Hattaa** (*even*), 4. **laylaa** (*Layla*)

15: GRAMMATICAL ENDINGS WITH -n

There are three **tanwiin** (double) short vowel endings in Arabic, **tanwiin 'al-fatH**, **tanwiin 'aD-Damm**, and **tanwiin 'al-kasr**. **tanwiin 'al-fatH** and **tanwiin 'al-kasr** are written like a pair of the short vowels, and **tanwiin 'aD-Damm** is like a **Damma** with a kind of hook: ˊ (**-an**), ˮ (**-un**), and ˌ (**-in**). Notice that they're all pronouncedwith -n. These symbols all typically occur above the last letter of a word, and they're used to show that a noun or adjective is indefinite. The distinction between these three symbols has to do with grammatical case, or the function of a noun in a sentence, for example as subject, direct object, possessive, or object of a preposition. The **tanwiin 'al-fatH** is also used in many common expressions. It usually appears before an **'alif** ـا / ا except when words end in **taa' marbuTaa** ة or **'alif hamza** اء. Notice that the hidden **t** of ة is pronounced if a **tanwiin** ending follows it.

a (male) student	Taaliban	طَالِبًا
thank you	shukraan	شُكْرًا
a (female) professor	'ustadhatan	أُسْتَاذَةً
evening	masaa'an	مَسَاءً
a girl	bintun	بِنْتٌ
beautiful	jamiilatin	جَمِيلَةٍ

READING PRACTICE 19

Practice reading the **tanwiin** ending in each of the following words.

1. كِتَابًا
2. كِتَابٌ
3. كِتَابٍ
4. جِدًّا

5. غَدَا

6. دائِماً

7. أَيْضاً

8. أَهْلاً وَسَهْلاً

Answers

1. **kitaaban** (*a book,* accusative), 2. **kitaabun** (*a book,* nominative), 3. **kitaabin** (*a book,* genitive), 4. **jiddan** (*very*), 5. **ghadan** (*tomorrow*), 6. **daa'iman** (*always*), 7. **'ayDan** (*also*), 8. **'ahlan wa sahlan** (*hello, welcome*)

16: OTHER SYMBOLS

There are three other symbols in written Arabic that you may come across, but because they're not very common, we'll only mention them in passing. **waSla** is an **'alif** with a symbol like a tailed **Damma** above it: آ. It occurs at the beginning of a definite word starting with **'al-** that follows a word ending in a vowel, and it serves to connect the two words. It means that the **'a** in **'al** is "absorbed" by the sound of the vowel before it.

| the United Arab Emirates | 'al imaaraati-l-xarabiyati-l-muttaHida | ٱلْإِمَارَاتِ ٱلْعَرَبِيَّةِ ٱلْمُتَّحِدة |
| the United States of America | 'al wilaayaati-l-muttaHidati-l-'amriikiya | ٱلْوِلَايَاتِ ٱلْمُتَّحِدَةِ ٱلْأَمِرِيكِيَّةِ |

Another symbol you may come across, especially in Koranic texts, is the **dagger 'alif**, which looks a bit like an apostrophe after **'alif**: ٱ. It's pronounced like a long **'alif**. And finally, the **'alif madda** looks like an **'alif** with a wavy line above it: آ. It occurs at the beginning or in the middle of a word, and it doubles the length of the **'alif**.

| Allah, God | 'allaah | الله |
| the Koran | 'al-qur'aan | ٱلْقُرْآن |

READING PRACTICE 20

Practice reading the following phrases, which include greetings and other useful vocabulary.

١. اللُّغة العَرَبيّة

٢. صَباح أَلخَيْر

٣. صَباح النُور

٤. مَساء أَلخَيْر

٥. مَساء النُور

٦. مَع السَلامَة

٧. أَسْكُن في ....

٨. بِالعَرَبي

٩. السَلامُ عَلَيكُم

١٠. تُسافِر بِالسَلامة

Answers

1. **'al-lugha 'al-xarabiyya** (*the Arabic language*), 2. **SabaaH 'al-khayr**
(*good morning*), 3. **SabaaH an-nuur** (*good morning*, response), 4. **masaa'**
'al-khayr (*good afternoon*), 5. **masaa' 'an-nuur** (*good afternoon*, response),
6. **maxa s-salaama** (*good-bye*), 7. **'askun fii ...** (*I live in ...*), 8. **bil-xarabii**
(*in Arabic*), 9. **'as-salaamu xalaykum** (*hello, peace be upon you*),
10. **tusaafir bis-salaama** (*have a good trip*)

READING PRACTICE 21

Now let's look at some simple sentences in Arabic. Take each one
slowly, and sound out each word as you read.

1. أنا أمريكيّ

2. هِيَ مُدَرِّسَة

3. ألمَدِينَة صَغيرَة .

4. الفُنْدُق كبير .

5. هُنَّ مِن مِصر .

6. مِن أَين أنْتُما؟

7. هذا كِتاب .

8. هذه طائِرَة .

9. هِيَ طَبيبَة .

10. هوَ مِصريّ و هِيَ أمْريكيّة .

11. ما هذا؟

12. هَلْ هَذا صَفّ اللُّغَة العَربيّة؟

Answers

1. **'anaa 'amriikiyy.** (*I'm American. [m.]*) 2. **hiya mudarrisa.** (*She's a teacher.*) 3. **'al-madiina Saghiira.** (*The city is small.*) 4. **'al-funduq kabiir.** (*The hotel is big.*) 5. **hunna min miSr.** (*They're [f.] from Egypt.*) 6. **min 'ayna 'antumaa?** (*Where are you two from?*) 7. **haadhaa kitaab.** (*This is a book.*) 8. **haadhihi Taa'ira.** (*This is an airplane.*) 9. **hiya Tabiiba.** (*She's a doctor.*) 10. **huwa miSriyy wa hiya 'amriikiyya.** (*He's Egyptian and she's American.*) 11. **maa haadha?** (*What's this?*) 12. **hal haadha Saff 'al-lugha 'al-xarabiyya?** (*Is this the Arabic class?*)

Part 3
Writing Arabic

Now that you've had plenty of practice reading Arabic, let's go back over the entire alphabet in small groups so that you can have more practice reading and you can also learn writing. You'll have a chance to practice writing the letters separately in all of their forms, and then you'll move on to words and sentences.

GROUP 1: LONG VOWELS

Let's start with long vowels. Remember that **'alif** and **waaw** are both non-connecting letters, so they only have two forms. Also remember that و and ي also represent the consonants **w** and **y**.

For the initial and independent forms of **'alif**, start at the top, and then simply write downwards. Add the **hamza** after you've written the stroke. For the medial and final forms, start the right connecting stroke on the line, move toward the left, and then draw the vertical stroke upwards.

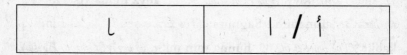

For **waaw**, start on the line at the base of the curve, and then draw the loop upwards and to the left, circling back to the right and down to meet the point where you started. Then keep writing to form the small tail below the line. If **waaw** is connected to a preceding letter, you'd simply start with the connecting stroke coming from the right. Writing **waaw** is similar to writing a lowercase *e*, but in the other direction.

ٮ	9

The letter **yaa'** is a little bit trickier. For the independent form, start a bit above the line, and then write a drawn-out *s*, with the lower hook extending below the line and then coming back up to cross it. Finally, add the two dots. The final form is similar, except you start with the right connecting stroke on the line, so final **yaa'** is flatter than independent **yaa'**.

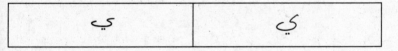

ـى	ـى

The initial and medial forms are very similar. For the initial form, start at a point above the line, and then write downwards to form the vertical stroke. When you reach the line, turn to the left to draw the left connecting stroke, finally adding the dots. For the medial form, start on the line with the right connecting stroke, writing to the left. Then draw the vertical stroke upwards, and double back down over it. When you reach the line again, turn left, and keep drawing the horizontal connecting stroke toward the left. Add the dots.

ـيـ	ـيـ

Practice writing these letters several times until you're comfortable with the movements needed to form them. Let's look at all of those forms together.

LETTER	SOUND	FINAL	MEDIAL	INITIAL	INDEPENDENT
'alif	a, aa	ل	ل	١ / أ	١ / أ
waaw	w, uu	و	و	و	و
yaa'	y, ii	ي	ـيـ	يـ	ي

WRITING PRACTICE 1

Practice writing the long vowels a few times on their own.

أ أ أ

ل ل ل

و و و

و و و

ي ي ي

يـ يـ يـ

ـيـ ـيـ ـيـ

ي ي ي

GROUP 2: SHORT VOWELS AND DIPHTHONGS

As you know, **fatHa** is written as a slash above the consonant: ´ ,
Damma is like a small hook: ٔ , and **kasra** is a slash below the
consonant: . . The vowels **fatHa** and **kasra** are straighforward, and
Damma is just like a miniature **waaw** written above the consonant.

WRITING PRACTICE 2

Practice writing each of these vowels in simple syllables with the
consonants و (**wa, wu, wi**) and ي (**ya, yu, yi**).

وَ وَ وَ

وُ وُ وُ

وِ وِ وِ

يَ يَ يَ

يُ يُ يُ

يِ يِ يِ

To write the diphthongs **aw** and **ay**, don't forget that you need **fatHa**
over the preceding consonant and then **sukuun** over وْ or يْ . The
sukuun is also used between consonants when there is no vowel
pronounced. **sukuun** is simply a small open circle.

WRITING PRACTICE 3

Practice writing diphthongs in the syllables يَوْ (**yaw**) and وَيْ (**way**).
Because this is the first time you'll be writing two letters together, it's
appropriate to point out that when you write Arabic words, you
should first write the main strokes of all the letters in the word,
and when you're done with the word, go back and add dots, short
vowels, or **sukuun**. This is just like written English; you go back to
cross your t's and dot your i's only after the whole word is written.

يَوْ يَوْ يَوْ

وَيْ وَيْ وَيْ

Don't forget that words that begin with a short vowel sound begin
with an **'alif** and **hamza** in written Arabic. The **hamza** in this
position is written like a small backwards 2. أَ is pronounced **'a**, أُ is
pronounced **'u**, and إِ is pronounced **'i**.

WRITING PRACTICE 4

Write **'alif** with each of the three short vowels.

أَ أَ أَ

أُ أُ أُ

إِ إِ إِ

GROUP 3: ب, ت, AND ث

Remember that the consonants **ب b,** **ت t,** and **ث th** differ from one another only in the number and placement of dots. These letters all sit on the line, and the dots are added above or below it. As always, start writing from the right. For the independent and final forms, form a wide shallow bowl, then add the dot(s).

ثـ	تـ	بـ
ـثـ	ـتـ	ـبـ

For the initial forms, start at the top of the vertical stroke on the right, move your pen down, then write the horizontal connecting stroke leftwards. Then finally add the dot(s). These letters are written exactly alike, but, of course, the dots are different.

ثـ	تـ	بـ

For the medial forms, start with the right horizontal connecting stroke, then move upwards to draw the vertical stroke. Then double back down over it, finishing with the left connecting stroke. Finally, add the dot(s).

ـثـ	ـتـ	ـبـ

Practice forming these letters several times, writing them over and over again until you're comfortable with the motion. Let's look at all of the forms together.

LETTER	SOUND	FINAL	MEDIAL	INITIAL	INDEPENDENT
baa'	b	ـب	ـبـ	بـ	ب
taa'	t	ـت	ـتـ	تـ	ت
thaa'	th	ـث	ـثـ	ثـ	ث

WRITING PRACTICE 5

Practice writing each of the forms separately.

ب ب ب

بـ بـ بـ

بـ بـ بـ

ـب ـب ـب

ت ت ت

تـ تـ تـ

ـتـ ـتـ ـتـ

ـت ـت ـت

ث ث ث

ثـ ثـ ثـ

ـثـ ـثـ ـثـ

ـث ـث ـث

WRITING PRACTICE 6

Now, let's practice writing syllables with these letters and the vowels you've learned. Write out each of the following syllables, and pronounce it aloud. Say whether each letter is independent, initial, medial, or final.

بَ .1

تا .2

ـتِ .3

ـتُ .4

ـثَ .5

بي .6

ـتو .7

ثُ .8

ـبِ .9

ـثِ .10

Answers

1. **ba** (independent), 2. **taa** (initial), 3. **ti** (medial), 4. **tu** (medial), 5. **tha** (final), 6. **bii** (initial), 7. **tuu** (medial), 8. **thu** (initial), 9. **bi** (medial), 10. **thi** (final).

WRITING PRACTICE 7

Let's move on to practice some actual Arabic words, using only the
consonants and vowels that you've learned so far. Remember to
write the body of each word first, and then, when you're done, to go
back and add the vowels and **sukuun**. Pronounce each word aloud
as you write it.

١. بَابْ

٢. أَبْ

٣. بَيْت

٤. بِ

٥. بُيوتْ

٦. تَابوت

٧. ثَبَتَ

٨. ثابِتْ

Answers

1. **baab** (*door*), 2. **'aab** (*father*), 3. **bayt** (*house*), 4. **bi** (*in, at, on, with*),
5. **buyuut** (*houses*), 6. **taabuut** (*coffin, casket*), 7. **thabata** (*he stood firm*),
8. **thaabit** (*fixed, firm*)

GROUP 4: ج، ح، AND خ

The consonants ج j, ح H, and خ kh are another trio that differ only in the placement (or presence) of a dot. To write the independent forms, start a bit above the line and draw a small wave down and toward the right, almost like you're writing the number 2. When you reach the line, turn to the left and draw the rounded tail stroke below the line. This motion is also similar to writing the number 2, except that the tail stroke is much larger, is rounded, and goes below the line. For ج, add a dot inside the tail, and for خ, add it on top.

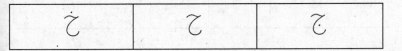

For the final forms, start in the same way, but then pick up your pen and write the connecting stroke from the right in a separate motion, meeting where you left off the first line. Then, from the same point, draw the tail stroke below the line.

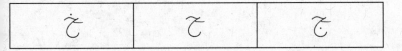

The initial and medial forms don't have the tail stroke. Start at the top of the wave shape above the line. In the medial form, you'll already have drawn a connecting stroke from the previous letter, and you'll meet this point with your pen. In the intial form, of course, there won't be any connecting stroke on the right. Then, write across the line to the left, forming the left connecting stroke.

ـِج	ـج	ـجـ
ـِح	ـح	ـح

LETTER	SOUND	FINAL	MEDIAL	INITIAL	INDEPENDENT
jiim	j	ـج	ـجـ	جـ	ج
Haa'	H	ـح	ـحـ	حـ	ح
khaa'	kh	ـخ	ـخـ	خـ	خ

WRITING PRACTICE 8

Practice the four forms of each letter separately.

$$\begin{array}{ccc} ج & ج & ج \end{array}$$

$$\begin{array}{ccc} خـ & خـ & خـ \end{array}$$

$$\begin{array}{ccc} ـحـ & ـحـ & ـحـ \end{array}$$

$$\begin{array}{ccc} خ & خ & خ \end{array}$$

$$\begin{array}{ccc} ح & ح & ح \end{array}$$

$$\begin{array}{ccc} ـح & ـح & ـح \end{array}$$

ح ح ح

ح ح ح

خ خ خ

ﺤ ﺤ ﺤ

ﺨ ﺨ ﺨ

خ خ خ

WRITING PRACTICE 9

Once again, let's practice reading and writing syllables with these letters and the vowels you've learned. Write and pronounce each syllable, and also say whether the consonant is in its initial, medial, final, or independent form.

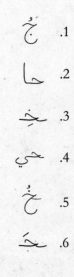

ﺡ .1

ﻂ .2

ﺨ .3

ﺤ .4

ﺡ .5

ﺨ .6

7. حَجِي

8. خُ

9. خَ

10. خِي

Answers

1. **ju** (independent), 2. **Haa** (initial), 3. **khi** (medial), 4. **Hii** (medial),
5. **khu** (final), 6. **ja** (medial), 7. **jii** (medial), 8. **khu** (independent),
9. **Hu** (final), 10. **khii** (medial)

WRITING PRACTICE 10

And here are some more words that use the letters that you've
learned to write so far. Again, don't forget to write the entire word
before you go back and add the short vowels, the dots, or **sukuun**.

1. أُخْـت

2. جِباب

3. جَنْج

4. جِيـب

5. حَبِيب

6. مُبَاجِب

7. حِجَاج

8. حَيْثُ

9. خَبَبْ

10. خَبُثَ

11. خَبِيثْ

12. وُجُوبْ

Answers

1. **'ukht** (*sister*), 2. **jibaab** (*jubbahs, a type of garment*), 3. **jabH** (*beehive*),
4. **jiip** (*jeep*), 5. **Habiib** (*sweetie, love*), 6. **HubaaHib** (*fireflies*), 7. **Hijaaj**
(*argument, debate*), 8. **Haythu** (*where, since*), 9. **khabab** (*trot*),
10. **khabutha** (*to be bad, wicked*), 11. **khabiith** (*evil, wicked*),
12. **wujuub** (*obligation*)

GROUP 5: د, ذ, ر, AND ز

Now let's add four more consonants. The pairs د / ذ and ر / ز
obviously differ with respect to the presence of a dot, but they're all
similar in that they're non-connecting letters, so they only have two
forms each. Note that د and ذ sit on top of the line, while ر and ز
extend below it. And don't forget that ذ is *th* as in *this* or *the*, not *th*
as in *think* or *three*, which is written ث.

The indepent and initial forms of د and ذ are simply small hooks
sitting on the line. The letter ذ has a dot over it. Because these letters
are non-connectors, you'd stop writing before adding any letters
afterwards.

ذ	ذ

To write the medial and final forms, start with the right connecting stroke on the line, write toward the left, curve upwards with a slanted stroke, and then double back over it. When you reach the line again, continue writing the horizontal connecting stroke toward the left.

ـذ	ـذ

The initial and independent forms of ر and ز are simply hooks that start above the line and then curve down and across it toward the left.

ز	ر

The medial and final forms begin with the right connecting stroke. Simply draw a straight line, and then turn upwards for the part of the letters that go above the line. Then double back down toward the line, and finish with a gentle hook toward the left.

ـز	ـر

Here are all of the forms.

LETTER	SOUND	FINAL	MEDIAL	INITIAL	INDEPENDENT
daal	d	ـد	ـد	د	د
dhaal	dh	ـذ	ـذ	ذ	ذ
raa'	r	ـر	ـر	ر	ر
zaay	z	ـز	ـز	ز	ز

WRITING PRACTICE 11

Practice writing the forms of these letters on their own. Add short vowels and say the syllables aloud as you write.

WRITING PRACTICE 12

Practice writing syllables with these letters and the vowels you've learned. Write and pronounce each syllable, and also say which form the consonant is in. Because these letters are non-connectors, there are only two options: initial/independent or medial/final.

دِ .1

زَ .2

ذِي .3

رُ .4

زَا .5

دِي .6

رَ .7

ذُو .8

رَا .9

أَد .10

Answers

1. **di** (initial/independent), 2. **za** (medial/final), 3. **dhii** (medial/final), 4. **ru** (initial/independent), 5. **zaa** (medial/final), 6. **dii** (initial/independent), 7. **ra** (medial/final), 8. **dhuu** (medial/final), 9. **raa** (initial/independent), 10. **'ad** (medial/final)

WRITING PRACTICE 13

And now practice pronouncing and writing these words.

1. بَحْر

2. بُدُوز

3. تَرْدِيدْ

4. رادار

5. راجَوات

6. خَرَجَ

7. خَدِزْ

8. حَرِجْ

9. إِنْتِراب

10. ذَبْذَبَ

11. ذَرِبْ

12. ذَوات

13. رَوْد

14. زَجَرَ

15. زُيُوتْ

16. زَوَر

17. زَوَاج

18. زِيِر

Answers

1. **baHr** (*sea*), 2. **buduur** (*full moons*), 3. **tardiid** (*repetition*), 4. **raadaar** (*radar*), 5. **raajawaat** (*rajas, Indian princes*), 6. **kharaja** (*he left*), 7. **khadir** (*numb*), 8. **Harij** (*confined*), 9. **'iHtiraab** (*struggle*), 10. **dhabdhaba** (*he swung, he dangled*), 11. **dharib** (*sharp*), 12. **dhawaat** (*essences, natures*), 13. **rawd** (*exploration*), 14. **zajara** (*he drove back*), 15. **zuyuut** (*oils*), 16. **zawar** (*slant*), 17. **zawaaj** (*marriage*), 18. **ziir** (*large water jars*)

WRITING PRACTICE 14

Connect the following letters to form words, and say the words aloud.

1. بَ + زَ + ر

2. خَ + زِ + ج

3. أ + حَ + د

4. خَ + د + ي + د

5. حَ + زَ + ا + ر

6. ذَ + ا + ت

7. ذَ + ا + ب

Answers

1. بَذَر (**badhar**, *seeding*), 2. خَرْج (**kharj**, *expenditure*), 3. أَحَد ('**aHad**, *someone*), 4. جَديد (**jadiid**, *new*), 5. حَذار (**Hadhaar**, *beware*), 6. ذَات (**dhaat**, *ego*), 7. ذَاب (**dhaab**, *melted*)

GROUP 6: س AND ش

Now let's add two more similar-looking consonants, س **s** and ش **sh**. In the independent and final forms, start on the right, and draw a series of three vertical strokes, like a lowercase *w*. For the independent form, you'll start at the top of the first stroke, but for the final form, you'll begin with a right connecting stroke on the line. At the last vertical stroke, when you double back down, extend below the line and draw a bowl-shaped tail.

ـس	س
ـش	ش

The intial and medial forms lack the final loop, so they look like a *w* sitting on the line.

ـسـ	سـ
ـشـ	شـ

Here are all the forms together.

LETTER	SOUND	FINAL	MEDIAL	INITIAL	INDEPENDENT
siin	s	ـس	ـسـ	سـ	س
shiin	sh	ـش	ـشـ	شـ	ش

WRITING PRACTICE 15

Practice writing each form of these letters separately, adding the short vowels and saying each syllable aloud.

س س س

سـ سـ سـ

ـسـ ـسـ ـسـ

ـس ـس ـس

ش ش ش

شـ شـ شـ

ـشـ ـشـ ـشـ

ـش ـش ـش

WRITING PRACTICE 16

And here are a few more words to practice what you've learned so far.

1. سَادِس

2. سُورِيا

3. سَبَحَت

4. سِياسِي

5. شَاي

6. شَرِبْتُ

7. أَسْوَد

8. دَرَسْتُ

9. تَشَاوَرَ

10. شَيْب

11. شَيْخْ

12. أَشْجَر

13. سَادَاتْ

14. سُوس

Answers

1. **saadis** (*sixth*), 2. **suuriyaa** (*Syria*), 3. **sabaHat** (*she swam*),
4. **siyaasiyy** (*political*), 5. **shaay** (*tea*), 6. **sharibtu** (*I drank*), 7. **'aswad**
(*black*), 8. **darastu** (*I studied*), 9. **tashaawara** (*he consulted*), 10. **shayb**
(*gray hair, old age*), 11. **shaykh** (*sheikh*), 12. **'ashjar** (*wooded*),
13. **saadaat** (*master, sir, honorable*), 14. **suus** (*licorice*)

GROUP 7: ظ AND ص, ض, ط

Now let's look at the "emphatic" consonants, **S**, **D**, **T**, and **DH**.
Notice that they all have a "hump" and that they come in two pairs
that differ only in the presence of a dot.

Let's start with ص and ض. For the independent and final forms,
start in middle of the letter, drawing the hump up and towards the
right. Then loop back down to the line and draw on the line back
towards the point where you began. Keep drawing past that point,
and then draw a small vertical stroke upwards, and finally double
back down, cross the line, and draw a bowl-shaped tail.

ـص	ص
ـض	ض

The intial and medial forms are written in the same way, except they
don't include the tail.

ـصـ	ـصـ
ـضـ	ـضـ

The letters ط and ظ are formed in the same way. Start in the middle, at the base of the hump, and then draw upwards and toward the right. Then come back along the horizontal line, meeting up with and continuing past the point where you began. Then just add a large vertical stroke. All of the forms look very similar.

ط	ط
ظ	ظ

Here are all the forms of these letters.

LETTER	SOUND	FINAL	MEDIAL	INITIAL	INDEPENDENT
Saad	S	ـص	ـصـ	صـ	ص
Daad	D	ـض	ـضـ	ضـ	ض
Taa'	T	ـط	ـطـ	طـ	ط
DHaa'	DH	ـظ	ـظـ	ظـ	ظ

WRITING PRACTICE 17

Practice writing these letters in all their forms separately. Add short vowels, and practice pronouncing the syllables aloud. Don't forget that these consonants give a very deep quality to the vowels around them.

ﺺ ﺺ ﺺ

ﺺ ﺺ ﺺ

ﺼ ﺼ ﺼ

ﺻ ﺻ ﺻ

ﺾ ﺾ ﺾ

ﺾ ﺾ ﺾ

ﻀ ﻀ ﻀ

ﺿ ﺿ ﺿ

ﻂ ﻂ ﻂ

ﻂ ﻂ ﻂ

ﻄ ﻄ ﻄ

ﻃ ﻃ ﻃ

ﻆ ﻆ ﻆ

ﻆ ﻆ ﻆ

ﻈ ﻈ ﻈ

ﻈ ﻈ ﻈ

ﻇ ﻇ ﻇ

WRITING PRACTICE 18

Practice writing these words.

1. صَاحِب

2. صَبَاح

3. صَحِيح

4. ضَبَطَ

5. ضَجِرَت

6. إِضْرَار

7. طَبِيب

8. طَبْخ

9. بَطَاطِس

10. حِظَار

11. حَظِيظ

12. حَاضِر

13. تَفَاطُب

14. وَسَط

1. **SaaHib** (*owner*), 2. **SabaaH** (*morning*), 3. **SaHiiH** (*true*),
4. **DabaTa** (*he grabbed*), 5. **Dajirat** (*she was angry*), 6. **'iDraar** (*harm, injury*),
7. **Tabiib** (*doctor [m.]*), 8. **Tabkh** (*cooking*), 9. **baTaaTis** (*potatoes*),
10. **HiDHaar** (*partition, screen*), 11. **HaDHiiDH** (*lucky*), 12. **HaaDir**
(*present, in attendance*), 13. **takhaaTub** (*discussion*), 14. **wasaT** (*middle*)

WRITING PRACTICE 19

Connect the following letters to form words.

1. ح + ظّ

2. صَ + ا + ح + ب

3. صَ + ر + ي + ر

4. ضَ + ر + س

5. ظَ + ب + ي

Answers

1. حَظّ (**HaDHDH**, *luck*), 2. صَاحِب (**SaaHib**, *owner*), 3. صَرير
(**Sariir**, *creak, chirp*), 4. ضَرْس (**Dars**, *molar*), 5. ظَبِي (**DHabii**, *deer*)

GROUP 8: ع AND غ

The pair ع **x** and غ **gh** are again only different in the placement of a
dot over غ **gh**. But notice that both of these letters have forms that
look quite different depending on where they are in a word, and only
the final and independent forms have tails.

For the independent forms, start above the line, and draw a backwards 3 so that the middle point sits on the line and the tail hook is wider than the top hook and extends below the line.

For the final forms, begin with the connecting stroke on the right, and then draw a small loop over the line and toward the right. Curve back down across the line, and draw the tail toward the left, and then curve back toward the right.

The initial forms start above the line, as a hook that opens toward the right, almost like a *c*. Curve down toward the line, and then draw the connecting line toward the left.

The medial forms are like loops, but the tops are flattened.

Here are all the forms together.

LETTER	SOUND	FINAL	MEDIAL	INITIAL	INDEPENDENT
xayn	x	ح	ح	ح	ع
ghayn	gh	ح	ح	ح	ع

WRITING PRACTICE 20

Practice each of the forms of these letters.

ع ع ع

ع ع ع

عـ عـ عـ

عـ عـ عـ

غ غ غ

غ غ غ

غـ غـ غـ

غـ غـ غـ

WRITING PRACTICE 21

Here are some more words to practice the letters that you've learned so far.

1. عَرَبِي

2. عَرُوس

3. أَعزَب

4. رَبِيع

5. صِرَاع

6. تَاسِع

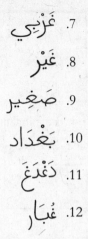

7. غَرْبِي

8. غَيْر

9. صَغِير

10. بَغْدَاد

11. دَغْدَغَ

12. غُبَار

Answers

1. **xarabiyy** (*Arabic*), 2. **xaruus** (*bride*), 3. **'axzab** (*single*), 4. **rabiix** (*spring*), 5. **Siraax** (*struggle*), 6. **taasix** (*ninth*), 7. **gharbiyy** (*western*), 8. **ghayr** (*not*), 9. **Saghiir** (*small*), 10. **baghdaad** (*Baghdad*), 11. **daghdagha** (*he tickled*), 12. **ghubaar** (*dust*)

GROUP 9: ق AND ف

The pair ف **f** and ق **q** differ in the number of dots they have and also in where they are positioned relative to the line. Notice that ق crosses below the line, while ف remains on it.

To write the independent and final forms, start either on the line or with the right connecting stroke, and draw a small loop up and around to the right. Then come back down to the line. For ف, continue straight on the line and form a small hook. For ق, come down past the line and draw a bowl-shaped tail.

ـڧ	ف
ـۊ	ۊ

For the initial and medial forms, just draw a small loop sitting on the line. In these positions, the letters only differ in the number of dots.

ـفـ	ف
ـقـ	ق

Here are all the forms together.

LETTER	SOUND	FINAL	MEDIAL	INITIAL	INDEPENDENT
faa'	f	ـف	ـفـ	ف	ف
qaaf	q	ـق	ـقـ	ق	ق

WRITING PRACTICE 22

Practice writing the forms of ق and ف on their own.

ف ف ف

ف ف ف

ڧ ڧ ڧ

ـف ـف ـف

ق ق ق

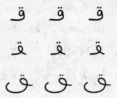

WRITING PRACTICE 23

And now practice writing words that include ف, ق, and other letters that you know.

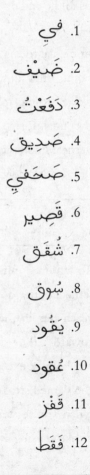

1. فِي

2. ضَيْف

3. دَفَعْتُ

4. صَدِيق

5. صَحَفِي

6. قَصِير

7. شُقَق

8. سُوق

9. يَقُود

10. عُقود

11. قَفْز

12. فَقَط

1. **fii** (*in*), 2. **Dayf** (*guest*), 3. **dafaxtu** (*I paid*), 4. **Sadiiq** (*friend*), 5. **SaHafiyy** (*journalist*), 6. **qaSiir** (*short*), 7. **shuqaq** (*apartments*), 8. **suuq** (*market*), 9. **yaquud** (*he leads*), 10. **xuquud** (*contracts*), 11. **qafz** (*jumping*), 12. **faqaT** (*only*)

GROUP 10: ك, ل, م, AND ن

Now let's add four more consonants to the list, which almost brings us to the end of the alphabet. We'll start with ك **k**, which has a small *s*-like stroke in its independent and final forms, but not in its initial or medial forms. To write the independent form, start at the top right point, draw down toward the line, and then draw toward the left along the line, forming a small upward hook at the very end. To write the final form, start with the right connecting stroke, draw the vertical line upwards, and then come back down, continuing as you did for the independent form. Add the small *s*.

To write the initial form, start with a stroke that's slanted toward the left, and draw down toward the line in a rightward motion. When you reach the line, level the stroke off and write the horizontal stroke toward the left. The medial form is written in a similar way, except you begin with the right connecting stroke, draw the slanted stroke, and then come back down along it. In both cases, when you've written the whole word, add another slanted vertical stroke starting at the top, moving toward the right.

خ	خ

Now let's look at ل, which has a hook extending below the line in the independent and final forms, but not in the initial and medial forms. For the independent form, simply write a *j* (without the dot, and starting higher above the line). For the final form, you'd begin with the right connecting stroke, draw the vertical upwards, then trace back down along it, and continue with the tail hook.

ل	ل

The intial and medial forms are very similar as well, except, of course, in where you start to write. Neither one has the hook that extends below the line.

ل	ل

The written forms of م all involve a small loop. For the independent form, start on the line, and draw a small loop upwards and toward the left, circling around toward the right, and then back down to the line. When you reach the line, draw a straight line toward the left, and then drop off to extend a tail that hangs down under the line. The final form is written in the same way, although you'd of course start with the right connecting stroke from the previous letter.

م	م

For the initial form, start in the same place and draw your loop, but don't draw the dangling tail line. The medial form is identical, but it begins with a right connecting stroke.

ـمـ	ـم

And finally, the letter ن is very similar to ب. In its independent and final forms, though, the bowl shape drops below the line. And, of course, the dot is above the line, rather than below it.

ـن	ن

The initial and medial forms of ن are really just like ب, although again there's a single dot above the letter rather than below it.

ـنـ	نـ

Let's look at all of those forms one more time.

LETTER	SOUND	FINAL	MEDIAL	INITIAL	INDEPENDENT
kaaf	k	ـك	ـكـ	كـ	ك
laam	l	ـل	ـلـ	لـ	ل
miim	m	ـم	ـمـ	مـ	م
nuun	n	ـن	ـنـ	نـ	ن

WRITING PRACTICE 24

Practice writing all the forms of these four consonants on their own, and then add short vowels and say the syllables aloud.

كَ كَ كَ

كَ كَ كَ

كَ كَ كَ

كَ كَ كَ

لَ لَ لَ

لَ لَ لَ

لَ لَ لَ

لَ لَ لَ

مَ مَ مَ

مـ مـ مـ

ـمـ ـمـ ـمـ

مـ مـ مـ

نَ نَ نَ

نَ نَ نَ

ـذ ـذ ـذ

ـن ـن ـن

WRITING PRACTICE 25

Practice writing the following words, which use a good mix of all the
letters we've covered so far.

1. لَحْم

2. لَيَالِي

3. كُرْسِي

4. نَعَم

5. مَشْرِق

6. كَثِير

7. مُدُن

8. قَلَم

9. سَاكِن

10. مِسْمَار

11. لَكِن

12. انَا

13. عِلْم

14. أَكَلْتُ

15. مَطَار

16. رِيَال

17. إِسْمُكَ

18. جَمِيل

Answers

1. **laHm** (*meat*), 2. **layaalii** (*nights*), 3. **kursii** (*chair*), 4. **naxam** (*yes*),
5. **mashriq** (*east*), 6. **kathiir** (*many*), 7. **mudun** (*cities*), 8. **qalam** (*pen*),
9. **saakin** (*resident*), 10. **mismaar** (*nail*), 11. **lakin** (*but*), 12. **'anaa** (*I*),
13. **xilm** (*knowledge*), 14. **'akaltu** (*I ate*), 15. **maTaar** (*airport*),
16. **riyaal** (*riyal*), 17. **'ismuka** (*your name*), 18. **jamiil** (*beautiful*)

GROUP 11: ه AND ة

Now let's look at ه **h**, which is the last consonant, and the similar-looking ة **a**, which is not a consonant but rather a short vowel pronounced just like **fatHa**. We'll start with ه, whose four forms look rather different from one another. The independent form is a simple open circle that sits on the line. The final form is similar, but it begins with the right connecting stroke. Draw a straight line up from the connecting stroke, and then form a rounded *c*-shape to the left, attached to the vertical stroke. Final ه winds up looking something like a lowercase cursive *a*, but it's written in the opposite direction.

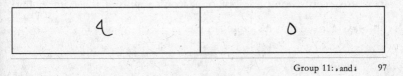

Before we go on to the other forms of ه, it's worth pointing out that if you simply add two dots to these letters, you have ة, or **taa' marbuuTa**.

ة	ة

Remember that **taa' marbuuTa** (tied **t**) is a very typical feminine ending in Arabic, pronounced exactly the same as **fatHa**. It has no medial or initial forms, because it only occurs at the end of words. The independent form is used when it follows a non-connecting letter. This letter is called **taa' marbuuTa** because in certain enviroments the "hidden" **t** is pronounced. But that never affects how it is written.

Now let's look at the initial and medial forms of ه. To form initial ه, write a leftward-facing loop on the line, like a backwards *c*. Then form a small loop within the *c*, and continue with the connecting stroke on the line moving toward the left. Medial ه looks something like the number 8, with its center resting on the line. Start with the connecting stroke on the right, and then draw the upper loop, first moving up and toward the left, then circling to the right and coming back down to the center point. Then continue below the line and draw the mirror image, first down and toward the left, and then toward the right and back up to the center point. Then just continue along the line for your left connecting stroke. Describing this action in words seems complex, but once you've written the letter a few times, you'll see that it's quite simple.

ـﻫ	ﻩ

Now let's look at all the forms of these two letters once again.

LETTER	SOUND	FINAL	MEDIAL	INITIAL	INDEPENDENT
haa'	h	ـﻪ	ـﻬـ	ﻫـ	ﻩ
taa' marbuuTa	a	ـﺔ			ﺓ

WRITING PRACTICE 26

Practice writing the forms of these letters.

ﻩ

ﻫـ

ـﻫـ

ـﻪ

ﺓ

ـﺔ

WRITING PRACTICE 27

Now practice writing words with these letters.

هذا .1

هَذِهِ .2

٣. هُنَاك

٤. ظَهْر

٥. جَامِعة

٦. غُرْفة

٧. كُرة

٨. فَهِمْت

٩. أَذهَب

١٠. مَدِينة

١١. زَهْرة

١٢. عَهْد

Answers

1. **haadhaa** (*this [m.]*), 2. **haadhihi** (*this [f.]*), 3. **hunaak** (*there*), 4. **DHahr** (*back*), 5. **jaamixa** (*university*), 6. **ghurfa** (*room*), 7. **kura** (*ball*), 8. **fahimt** (*I understood*), 9. **'adhhab** (*I go*), 10. **madiina** (*city*), 11. **zahra** (*blossom*), 12. **xahd** (*era*)

Now you've learned how to write all of the consonants, the long vowels, the short vowels and **taa' marbuuTa**, and the diphthongs and **sukuun**. In the reading section, you learned that there are also some more special forms, so let's practice writing them now.

GROUP 12: **shadda, laam-'alif**, THE DEFINITE ARTICLE

The symbol **shadda** looks like a 3 on its side, and it's written above consonants to show that they should be pronounced longer. **shadda** is like a short vowel in that it's not usually written. But the combination letter **laam-'alif** is written. It's pronounced just as you'd expect, as ﺍ following ﻝ, or **laa**. To write its isolated form, start above the line, and draw a slanted stroke down and toward the left. When you get to the line, change direction, and then loop back up, making a small circle and extending back up toward the left. Isolated **laam-'alif** should look something like a rabbit's head, if you have a little imagination! This letter is a non-connector, so the isolated form is also the intial form. The final form starts out like a final ﻝ, but there's no tail that extends below the line. Start with the right connecting stroke, and draw the vertical stroke up, and then back down again. Draw a small tail that sits on the line, and then add a slanted vertical stroke from the top left that meets the line at the same point where the vertical line does.

The order **'alif laam** is, of course, the definite article, ﺍﻟ. In writing and in speech, the article is attached to the word that follows it. There's nothing special about the way it's written. Simply start with ﺍ, which may have **hamza** and **fatHa** over it in fully voweled writing, and then draw initial ﻝ, because **'alif** is a non-connector. Don't forget that ﻝ is sometimes pronounced like the consonant that follows it, in the case of "sun" letters, but this never changes its spelling. But if the noun itself starts with a short vowel, it will be written as an **'alif**, so with the definite article the combination will be ﺍ + ﻝ + ﺍ. That will give you an **'alif**, and then a **laam-'alif**.

WRITING PRACTICE 28

Practice writing **shadda**, **laam-'alif**, and the definite article.

ﻻ ﻻ ﻻ

ﺃَﻝ ﺃَﻝ ﺃَﻝ

ﺃَﻝَﺀ ﺃَﻝَﺀ ﺃَﻝَﺀ

WRITING PRACTICE 29

Now practice writing these words.

1. سِتّة

2. مَمَرّ

3. حَمّام

4. كُلّ

5. لاحِق

6. سَلام

7. لازِم

8. طُلاب

9. أَلْبَيْت

10. أَلْرَجُل

11. أَلْيَوْم

12. أَلْسَبَب

13. أَلْإِسْم

14. أَلْأُخْت

15. أَلْأَوْلاد

Answers

1. **sitta** (*six*), 2. **mamarr** (*corridor*), 3. **Hammaam** (*bathroom*),
4. **kull** (*each*), 5. **laaHiq** (*later*), 6. **salaam** (*peace*), 7. **laazim** (*necessary*),
8. **Tulaab** (*students*), 9. **'al-bayt** (*the house*), 10. **'ar-rajul** (*the man*),
11. **'al-yawm** (*the day*), 12. **'as-sabab** (*the reason*), 13. **'al-'ism** (*the name*),
14. **'al-'ukht** (*the sister*), 15. **'al-'awlaad** (*the boys*)

13: hamza

You already know that words that begin with a short vowel are written
in Arabic with a **hamza,** which is written like a small backwards 2. and
sits on top of or below an **'alif.** The **'alif** itself isn't pronounced;
it's just a host for the short vowel. So, أَ is pronounced **'a** أُ is
pronounced **'u, 'u,** and إِ is pronounced **'i.**

WRITING PRACTICE 30

Practice writing a few words that begin with vowels.

1. أَنَا

2. إِبْن

3. أُخْت

4. أَرْبَعة

5. أُسْتاذة

6. إِجازة

7. أَمْريكي

8. إِمْتِحان

Answers

1. **'anaa** (*I*), 2. **'ibn** (*son*), 3. **'ukht** (*sister*), 4. **'arbaxa** (*four*), 5. **'ustaadha** (*professor [f.]*), 6. **'ijaaza** (*vacation*), 7. **'amriikii** (*American [m.]*), 8. **'imtiHaan** (*exam*)

As you saw in the reading section, **hamza** can also come in the middle of a word or at the end, where it may be written in a few different ways. We've already covered some generalizations about spelling with **hamza** in the reading section, so we won't review them here. If you need to go over them again, turn back to the reading section before you practice writing words with **hamza**.

WRITING PRACTICE 31

Practice writing these words with **hamza**.

1. إِمْرأَة

2. سَأَلَ

3. رَأْس

4. فأْرة

5. سَوُول

6. سُوُّل

7. تَرَوُّس

8. رُؤْية

9. عَائِلة

10. أُخَصَّيُّ

11. أَلجَزَائِر

12. رَئِيسي

13. طَائِرة

14. قِراءة

15. مَساء

16. نِساء

17. هَنَأً

Answers

1. **'imraa'a** (*woman*), 2. **sa'ala** (*he asked*), 3. **ra's** (*head*), 4. **fa'ra** (*mouse [f.]*),
5. **sa'uul** (*curious*), 6. **su'l** (*request, demand*), 7. **tara'us** (*management*),
8. **ru'ya** (*sight*), 9. **xaa'ila** (*family*), 10. **'akhaSSa'ii** (*specialist*),
11. **al-jazaa'ir** (*Algeria*), 12. **ra'iisii** (*main*), 13. **Taa'ira** (*airplane*),
14. **qiraa'a** (*reading*), 15. **masaa'** (*evening*), 16. **nisaa'** (*women*),
17. **hana'a** (*to be wholesome*)

14: 'alif maqSuura AND GRAMMATICAL ENDINGS WITH -n

As you learned in the reading section, **'alif maqSuura** is pronounced like a long **aa**, and it only occurs at the end of a word. It's written ﻯ, without dots. The grammatical endings with -**n**, or **tanwiin**, should give you no trouble writing, either.

WRITING PRACTICE 32

Practice writing the following words with **'alif maqSuura** and **tanwiin**.

1. إِلَى

2. حَكَى

3. شُكْرًا

4. بِنْتٌ

5. كِتَابٍ

Answers

1. **'ilaa** (*to*), 2. **Hakaa** (*told*), 3. **shukran** (*thank you*), 4. **bintun** (*a girl*), 5. **kitaabin** (*a book*)

WRITING PRACTICE 33

Now practice writing and pronouncing the following words.

1. هُوَ

2. هُنا

3. فِي مِصْر

4. تَتَكَلَّم

5. أَللُّغة

6. رَجُل و إِمْرَأة

7. أَلإِنْجليزيّة

8. بُيوت كَبيرة

9. صَباح ألْخَير

10. زَميل

Answers

1. **huwa** (*he*), 2. **hunaa** (*here*), 3. **fii miSr** (*in Egypt*), 4. **tatakallam** (*you speak*), 5. **al-lugha** (*the language*), 6. **rajul wa 'imra'a** (*a man and a woman*), 7. **al-'ingliiziyya** (*English*), 8. **buyuut kabiira** (*big houses*), 9. **SabaaH al-khayr** (*good morning*), 10. **zamiil** (*colleague*)

WRITING PRACTICE 34

Connect the following letters to form words.

1. ثِ + يْ + وَ + كُ

2. ش + و + مُ + قَ

3. قْ + ي + د + صَ

4. ن + كِ + لَ

5. ذ + ا + تَ + ش + أُ

6. ى + فَ + ش + تَ + ش + مُ

7. طَ + ا + بْ + عَ + ´

8. مْ + و + يَ

9. ة + لَ + ف + حَ

10. ´ + ا + رَ + ي + ثِ + كَ

11. ش + و + لُ + فُ

12. ب + و + زُ + ش + مَ

13. ض + ي + خِ + رَ

14. مَ + عَ

15. ا + نَ + لْ + كَ + أُ

Answers

1. كُوَيْتْ (**kuwayt**, *Kuwait*), 2. قَمُوسْ (**qamuus**, *dictionary*), 3. صَديقْ (**Sadiiq**, *friend*), 4. لَكِنْ (**lakin**, *but*), 5. أُسْتَاذْ ('**ustaadh**, *professor [m.]*), 6. مُسْتَشْفَى (**mustashfaa**, *hospital*), 7. طَبْعاً (**Tabxan**, *of course*), 8. يَوْمْ (**yawm**, *day*), 9. حَفْلَة (**Hafla**, *party*), 10. كَثيراً (**kathiiran**, *a lot*), 11. فُلُوسْ (**fuluus**, *money*), 12. مَشْرُوب (**mashruub**, *drink*), 13. رَخيصْ (**rakhiiS**, *cheap*), 14. مَعَ (**maxa**, *with*), 15. أَكَلْنَا ('**akalnaa**, *we ate*)

WRITING PRACTICE 35

Practice writing the following phrases that you saw earlier in the reading section.

1. اللُغة العَرَبيّة

2. صَباح الخَير

3. صَباح النُور

4. مَساء الخير

5. مَساء النُور

6. مَع السَلامة

7. أُسْكُن في

8. بِالعَرَبي

9. السَلامُ عَلَيكُم

10. تُسافِر بِالسَلامة

Answers

1. **'al-lugha 'al-xarabiyya** (*the Arabic language*), 2. **SabaaH 'al-khayr** (*good morning*), 3. **SabaaH 'an-nuur** (*good morning,* response), 4. **masaa' 'al-khayr** (*good afternoon*), 5. **masaa' 'an-nuur** (*good afternoon,* response), 6. **maxa 'as-salaama** (*good-bye*), 7. **'askun fii ...** (*I live in ...*), 8. **bil-xarabii** (*in Arabic*), 9. **'as-salaamu xalaykum** (*hello, peace be upon you*), 10. **tusaafir bis-salaama** (*have a safe trip*)

WRITING PRACTICE 36

Now practice writing those simple sentences you read earlier.

1. أَنا أَمريكيّ

2. هِيَ مُدَرِّسة.

3. اَلْمَدينة صَغيرة.

4. اَلْفُندُق كَبير.

5. هُنَّ مِن مِصْر.

6. مِن أَيَن أَنْتُما؟

7. هذا كِتاب.

8. هذه طائرة.

9. هِيَ طَبيبة.

10. هُوَ مِصْرِيّ و هِيَ امْريكيّة.

11. ما هَذا؟

12. هَلْ هَذا صَفّ اللُّغَة العَربيّة؟

Answers

1. **'anaa 'amriikiyy.** (*I'm American.* [*m.*]) 2. **hiya mudarrisa.** (*She's a teacher.*)
3. **'al-madiina Saghiira.** (*The city is small.*) 4. **'al-funduq kabiir.** (*The hotel is big.*)
5. **hunna min miSr.** (*They're* [*f.*] *from Egypt.*) 6. **min 'ayna 'antumaa?** (*Where are you two from?*) 7. **haadhaa kitaab.** (*This is a book.*) 8. **haadhihi Taa'ira.** (*This is an airplane.*) 9. **hiya Tabiiba.** (*She's a doctor.*) 10. **huwa miSriyy wa hiya 'amriikiyya.** (*He's Egyptian and she's American.*) 11. **maa haadha?** (*What's this?*) 12. **hal haadhaa Saff 'al-lugha 'al-xarabiyya?** (*Is this the Arabic class?*)

Part 4
Reading Passages

In this section you'll have the chance to put your Arabic reading skills to work by reading four of the fifteen dialogues featured in *Complete Arabic: The Basics*.

Probably the most difficult part of reading actual written Arabic is the fact that short vowels and many other helpful symbols, such as **sukuun**, **shadda**, and so on, are not usually included. To help you make this challenging transition, each dialogue appears twice,–first fully voweled, and then again in "natural" form, with only consonants and long vowels.

DIALOGUE 1
(Lesson 2 of *Complete Arabic: The Basics*)

السَّلَامُ عَلَيْكُمْ

كَرِيم : أَهْلاً وَ سَهْلاً!

كَمَال : أَهْلاً وَسَهْلاً!

كَرِيم : كَيْفَ الْحَالُ؟

كَمَال : الْحَمْدُ لله. وَ أَنْتَ، كَيْفَ الْحَالُ؟

كَرِيم : الْحَمْدُ لله.

السلام عليكم

كريم: أهلا وسهلا!

كمال: أهلا وسهلا!

كريم: كيف الحال؟

كمال: الحمد لله. وأنت، كيف الحال؟

كريم: الحمد لله.

'as-salaam xalaykum
kariim: 'ahlan wa sahlan!
kamaal: 'ahlan wa sahlan!
kariim: kayfa l-Haal?
kamaal: 'al-Hamdu lillaah. wa 'anta, kayfa l-Haal?
kariim: 'al-Hamdu lillaah.

Hello
Karim: *Hi!*
Kamal: *Hi!*
Karim: *How are you?*
Kamal: *I'm doing well. And you, how are you?*
Karim: *I'm doing well.*

DIALOGUE 2
(Lesson 6 of *Complete Arabic: The Basics*)

فِي الْفُنْدُق

مُوَظَّفُ الْإِسْتِقْبَالِ: صَبَاحُ الْخَيْرِ وَ مَرْحَبًا بِكِ إِلَى فُنْدُقِ السَّفَنْكْسِ.

جُولِي: صَبَاحُ النُّورِ، شُكْرًا. هَلْ لَدَيْكُمْ غُرْفَةٌ؟

مُوَظَّفُ الْإِسْتِقْبَالِ: نَعَمْ يَا سَيِّدَتِي. هَلْ تُرِيدِينَ غُرْفَةً لِشَخْصٍ وَاحِدٍ أَوْ غُرْفَةً لِشَخْصَيْنِ؟

جُولِي: غُرْفَةٌ لِشَخْصٍ، شُكْرًا.

مُوَظَّفُ الْإِسْتِقْبَالِ: لِكَمْ مِنْ لَيْلَةٍ؟

جُولِي: لِأَرْبَعَةِ لَيَالِي، مِنْ فَضْلِكَ.

مُوَظَّفُ الْإِسْتِقْبَالِ: غُرْفَةٌ بِحَمَّامٍ؟ بِدُشٍّ؟ أَوْ بِدُونِ حَمَّامٍ؟

جُولِي: بِحَمَّامٍ وَ دُشٍّ مِنْ فَضْلِكَ. هَلْ عِنْدَكُمْ قُطُورٌ؟

مُوَظَّفُ الْإِسْتِقْبَالِ: نَعَمْ يَا سَيِّدَتِي وَعِنْدَنَا خِدْمَةٌ لِلْغُرْفَةِ وَ مَطْعَمٌ لِلْغَدَاءِ وَ الْعَشَاءِ. عِنْدَكِ غُرْفَةٌ رَقْمٌ ثَلَاثُ مِائَةٍ وَأَرْبَعَةَ عَشَرَ فِي الطَّابِقِ الثَّالِثِ. الْغُرْفَةُ كَبِيرَةٌ وَ مُشْمِسَةٌ.

جُولِي: هَلِ الْغُرْفَةُ هَادِئَةٌ؟

مُوَظَّفُ الْإِسْتِقْبَالِ: نَعَمْ يَا سَيِّدَتِي. الْغُرْفَةُ هَادِئَةٌ.

جُولِي: هَذَا مُمْتَازٌ. أَنَا تَعْبَانَةٌ جِدًّا.

مُوَظَّفُ الْإِسْتِقْبَال: هَلْ كَانَ السَّفَرُ طَوِيلاً؟

جُولِي: نَعَمْ، مِنْ نُيُورْكْ.

مُوَظَّفُ الْإِسْتِقْبَال: أَنْتِ أَمْرِيكِيَّةٌ. تَتَكَلَّمِينَ عَرَبِيَّةً مُمْتَازَةً.

جُولِي: أَنَا مِنْ كَنَدَا وَ لَكِنْ جِئْتُ مِنْ نُيُورْكْ.

وَ شُكْرًا،الْعَرَبِيَّةُ لُغَةٌ صَعْبَةٌ وَ لَكِنْ جَدِيرَةٌ بِالْإِهْتِمَامِ.

في الفندق

موظّف الإستقبال: صباح الخير و مرحبا بك إلى فندق السّفنكس.

جولي: صباح النّور، شكرا. هل لديكم غرفة؟

موظّف الإستقبال: نعم يا سيّدتي. هل تريدين غرفة لشخص واحد أو غرفة لشخصين؟

جولي: غرفة لشخص، شكرا.

موظّف الإستقبال: لكم من ليلة؟

جولي: لأربعة ليالي ، من فضلك.

موظّف الإستقبال: غرفة بحمّام؟ بدشّ؟ أو بدون حمّام؟

جولي: بحمّام و دشّ من فضلك. هل عندكم فطور؟

موظّف الإستقبال: نعم يا سيّدتي وعندنا خدمة للغرفة و مطعم للغداء و العشاء. عندك غرفة رقم ثلاث مائة وأربعة عشر

في الطّابق الثّالث . الغرفة كبيرة و مشمسة .

جولي : هل الغرفة هادئة؟

موظّف الإستقبال : نعم يا سيّدتي . الغرفة هادئة .

جولي : هذا ممتاز . أنا تعبانة جدّا .

موظّف الإستقبال : هل كان السّفر طويلا؟

جولي : نعم، من نويورك .

موظّف الإستقبال : أنت أمريكيّة . تتكلّمين عربيّة ممتازة .

جولي : أنا من كندا و لكن جئت من نويورك .

و شكرا، العربيّة لغة صعبة و لكن جديرة بالإهتمام .

fi l-funduq	
muwaDHDHaf 'al-'istiqbaal:	SabaaH 'al-khayr, wa marHaban biki 'ilaa funduq sfinks.
julii:	SabaaH 'an-nuur. shukran. hal ladaykum ghurfa?
muwaDHDHaf 'al-'istiqbaal:	naxam, ya sayyidatii. hal turiidiina ghurfa li shakhS waaHid 'aw ghurfa li shakhSayni?
julii:	ghurfa li shakhS, shukran.
muwaDHDHaf 'al-'istiqbaal:	li kam min layl?
julii:	li 'arbaxat layaali, min faDlika.
muwaDHDHaf 'al-'istiqbaal:	ghurfa bi Hammaam? bi dush? 'aw biduun Hammaam?
julii:	bi Hammaam wa dush, min faDliki. hal xindakum fuTuur?
muwaDHDHaf 'al-'istiqbaal:	naxam, ya sayyidatii. wa xindanaa khidma li l-ghurfa wa maTxam li l-ghadaa' wa l-xashaa'. xindaki ghurfa raqm thalaatha mi'a wa

	'arbaxata 'ashar, fii T-Taabiq
	'ath-thaalith. 'al-ghurfa kabiira wa
	mushmisa.
julii:	hal 'al-ghurfa haadi'a?
muwaDHDHaf 'al-'istiqbaal:	naxam, ya sayyidatii. 'al-ghurfa
	haadi'a.
julii:	haadhaa mumtaaz. 'anaa
taxbaana jiddan.	
muwaDHDHaf 'al-'istiqbaal:	hal kaana 'as-safar Tawiilan?
julii:	naxam. min nuu yurk.
muwaDHDHaf 'al-'istiqbaal:	'anti 'amriikiyya. tatakallamiina
	xarabiyya mumtaaza.
julii:	'anaa min kanadaa, wa laakin
	ji'tu min nuu yurk. wa shukran.
	'al-xarabiyya lugha Saxba wa
	laakin jadiira bi l-'ihtimaam.

At the hotel

Clerk: Good morning, and welcome to the Hotel Sphinx.

Julie: Good morning. Thank you. Do you have a room?

Clerk: Yes, ma'am. Would you like a single or a double?

Julie: A single room, thank you.

Clerk: For how many nights?

Julie: For four nights, please.

Clerk: With a bathroom? With a shower? Or without a bathroom?

Julie: With a bathroom and shower, please. And do you have breakfast?

Clerk: Yes, ma'am. There is also room service and a restaurant for lunch and dinner. You'll be in room 314, on the third floor. It's big and sunny.

Julie: Is the room quiet?

Clerk: Yes, ma'am. The room is very quiet.

Julie: That's wonderful. I'm very tired.

Clerk: Was your trip long?

Julie: Yes. From New York.

Clerk: You're American. You speak excellent Arabic.

Julie: I'm from Canada, but I came from New York. And thank you. Arabic is a hard language, but very interesting.

DIALOGUE 3
(Lesson 10 of *Complete Arabic: The Basics*)

إِلَى الْأَرْبِعَاء

سَارَّة: هَلْ يُمْكِنُ أَنْ أَسْتَعْمِلَ الْهَاتِفَ؟

الْبَائِعُ: طَبْعًا.

سَارَّة: أَعْطِينِي بِطَاقَةً لِلْهَاتِفِ مِنْ فَضْلِكَ.

الْبَائِعُ: هَلْ تُرِيدِينَ بِطَاقَةً لِخَمْسَة دَنَانِير أَوْعَشَرَةَ دَنَانِير؟

سَارَّة: عَشَرَةَ دَنَانِيرِمِنْ فَضْلِكَ. هَلْ عِنْدَكَ دَلِيلُ الْهَاتِفِ؟

الْبَائِعُ: تَفَضَّلِي.

سَارَّة: شُكْرًا.

عَلَى الْهَاتِفِ

سَارَّة: آلُو، أُرِيدُ أَنْ أَتَكَلَّمَ مَعَ الطَّبِيبِ.

الْمُمَرِّضَةُ: آسِفَةٌ، هُوَ لَيْسَ هُنَا الآنَ. هَلْ تُرِيدِينَ أَنْ تَتْرُكِي خَبَرًا؟

سَارَّة: نَعَمْ، أُرِيدُ مَوْعِدًا مَعَ الطَّبِيبِ يَوْمَ الْخَمِيسِ. هَلْ هَذَا مُمْكِنٌ؟

الْمُمَرِّضَةُ: إِبْقَيْ عَلَى الْهَاتِفِ مِنْ فَضْلِكِ. هُوَ لَيْسَ هُنَا الْخَمِيسَ. يَذْهَبُ إِلَى إِرْبِد كُلَّ خَمِيسٍ، يَعْمَلُ فِي الْمُسْتَشْفَى هُنَاكَ. هَلِ الثَّلَاثَاءُ يُوَافِقُكِ؟

سَارَّة: أَنَا فِي الْمَكْتَبِ الثَّلَاثَاءَ وَأَنْتَهِي مِنْ الْعَمَلِ فِي اللَّيْلِ.

الْمُمَرِّضَةُ: هَلْ أَنْتِ فِي الْمَكْتَبِ الأربعاء؟

سَارَّة: الأربعاء جَيِّدٌ. أَيّ وَقْتٍ مِنْ فَضْلِكِ؟

الْمُمَرِّضَةُ: سَيَكُونُ هُنَاكَ فِي السَّاعَةِ الْوَاحِدَةِ.

سَارَّة: هَذَا جَيِّدٌ، شُكْرًا جَزِيلاً.

الْمُمَرِّضَةُ: إِلَى الأربعاءِ فِي السَّاعَةِ الْوَاحِدَةِ.

سَارَّة: شُكْرًا، مَعَ السَّلاَمَةِ.

الْمُمَرِّضَةُ: مَعَ السَّلاَمَةِ.

إلى الأربعاء

سارة: هل يمكن أن أستعمل الهاتف؟

البائع: طبعا.

سارة: أعطيني بطاقة للهاتف من فضلك.

البائع: هل تريدين بطاقة لخمسة دنانير أوعشرة دنانير؟

سارة: عشرة دنانيرمن فضلك. هل عندك دليل الهاتف؟

البائع: تفضلي.

سارة: شكرا.

على الهاتف

سارة: آلو، أريد أن أتكلم مع الطبيب.

الممرضة: آسفة، هو ليس هنا الآن. هل تريدين أن تتركي خبرا؟

سارة: نعم، أريد موعدا مع الطبيب يوم الخميس. هل هذا ممكن؟

الممرضة: إبقي على الهاتف من فضلك. هو ليس هنا يوم الخميس.

يذهب إلى إربد كل خميس، يعمل في المستشفى هناك.

هل الثلاثاء يوافقك؟

سارة: أنا في المكتب الثلاثاء وأنتهي من العمل في الليل.

الممرضة: هل أنت في المكتب الأربعاء؟

سارة: الأربعاء جيد. أي وقت من فضلك؟

الممرضة: سيكون هناك في الساعة الواحدة.

سارة: هذا جيد، شكرا جزيلا.

الممرضة: إلى الأربعاء في الساعة الواحدة.

سارة: شكرا، مع السلامة.

الممرضة: مع السلامة.

'ilaa l-'arbixaa'
sara:	hal yumkin 'an 'astaxmila l-haatif?
'al-baa'ix:	Tabxan.
sara:	'axTiinii biTaaqa li l-haatif min faDlika.

'al-baa'ix: hal turiidiina biTaaqa li khamsat diinaraat
                  'aw xashrat diinaraat?

sara: xashrat diinaraat min faDlika. hal xinda-
                  ka daliil 'al-haatif?

'al-baa'ix: tafaDDalii.

sara: shukran.

xalaa l-haatif

sara: 'allo. 'uriidu 'an 'atakallama maxa
                  T-Tabiib.

'al-mumarriDa: 'aasifa, huwa laysa hunaa l-'aan. hal
                  turiidiina 'an tatrukii khabaran?

sara: naxam. 'uriidu mawxidan maxa T-Tabiib
                  yawma l-khamiis. hal haadhaa mumkin?

'al-mumarriDa: 'ibqay xalaa l-haatif min faDliki. huwa
                  laysa hunaa l-khamiis. yadh-habu 'ilaa
                  'irbid kulla khamiis. yaxmalu fii l-mus-
                  tashfaa hunaaka. Hal 'ath-thulathaa'
                  yuwaafiquki?

sara: 'anaa fii l-maktab 'ath-thulathaa' wa
                  'antahii min 'al-xamal fii l-layl.

'al-mumarriDa: hal 'anti fii l-maktab 'al-'arbixaa'?

sara: 'al-'arbixaa' jayyid. 'ay waqt min faDlik?

'al-mumarriDa: sa-yakuunu hunaaka fii s-saaxa l-
                  waaHida.

sara: haadhaa jayyid. shukran jaziilan.

'al-mumarriDa: 'ilaa l-'irbixaa' fii s-saaxa l-waaHida.

sara: shukran. maxa 'as-salaama

'al-mumarriDa: maxa as-salaama.

See You Wednesday

Sara: Is it possible for me to use the phone?

Clerk: Of course.

Sara: Please give me a phone card.

Clerk: Would you like a card for five dinars or ten dinars?

Sara: Ten dinars, please. Do you have a phone book?

Clerk: Here you go.

Sara: Thank you.

On the Phone ...

Sara: Hello. I'd like to speak with the doctor.

Nurse: I'm sorry, but he's not in now. Would you like to leave a message?

Sara: Yes. I'd like an appointment with the doctor on Thursday. Is that
         possible?

Nurse: Please hold the line. He's not here on Thursday. He goes to Irbid
         on Thursdays. He works in the hospital there. Is Tuesday good
         for you?

Sara: I'm in the office on Tuesday, and I finish at night.

Nurse: Are you in the office on Wednesday?

Sara: Wednesday is good. What time, please?

Nurse: He's going to be here at one o'clock.

Sara: That's good. Thank you very much.

Nurse: See you Wednesday at one o'clock.

Sara: Thank you. Good-bye.

Nurse: Good-bye.

DIALOGUE 4

(Lesson 14 of *Complete Arabic: The Basics*)

أُرِيدُ أَنْ أَصْرِفَ مَائَةَ دُولَارٍ

مَارِي: أُرِيدُ أَنْ أَصْرِفَ دُولَارَاتٍ إِلَى دَرَاهِمَ.

أَمِينُ الْمَصْرِف: كَمْ مِنْ دُولَارٍ تُرِيدِينَ أَنْ تُصَرِّفِي؟

مَارِي: مَائَةَ دُولَارٍ مِنْ فَضْلِكَ.

أَمِينُ الْمَصْرِف: هَلْ عِنْدَكِ جَوَازُ سَفَرِكِ؟

مَارِي: نَعَمْ، هَا هُوَ.

أَمِينُ الْمَصْرِف: شُكْرًا، كَيْفَ تُرِيدِينَ الْفُلُوسَ؟

مَارِي: عَشَرَةَ أَوْرَاقٍ، مِنْ فَضْلِكَ.

أَمِينُ الْمَصْرِف: يَجِبُ الْإِمْضَاءُ هُنَا مِنْ فَضْلِكِ.

مَارِي: طَبْعًا.

أَمِينُ الْمَصْرِف: سَيِّدَتِي، لَمْ تَكْتُبِي رَقْمَ جَوَازِ السَّفَرِ.

مَارِي: عَفْوًا. لَمْ أَرَهُ فِي الْإِسْتَمَارَةِ، هَا هُوَ.

أَمِينُ الْمَصْرِف: شُكْرًا. تَفَضَّلِي.

مَارِي: شُكْرًا جَزِيلاً.

أريد أن أصرف مائة دولار

ماري: أريد أن أصرف دولارات إلى دراهم.

أمين المصرف: كم من دولار تريدين أن تصرّفي؟

ماري : مائة دولار من فضلك .

أمين المصرف : هل عندك جواز سفرك؟

ماري : نعم، ها هو .

أمين المصرف : شكرا، كيف تريدين الفلوس؟

ماري : عشرة أوراق، من فضلك .

أمين المصرف : يجب الإمضاء هنا من فضلك .

ماري : طبعا .

أمين المصرف : سيدتي، لم تكتبي رقم جواز السفر .

ماري : عفوا . لم أره في الإستمارة، ها هو .

أمين المصرف : شكرا . تفضّلي .

ماري : شكرا جزيلا .

mari:	'uriidu 'an 'aSrifa duulaaraat 'ilaa daraahim.
'amiin 'al-maSrif:	kam min duulaar turiidiina 'an tuSarrifii?
mari:	mi'at duulaar min faDlika.
'amiin 'al-maSrif:	hal xindaki jawaaz safariki?
mari:	naxam. haa huwa.
'amiin 'al-maSrif:	shukran. kayfa turiidiina l-fuluus?
mari:	xashrat 'awraaq min faDlika.
'amiin 'al-maSrif:	yajibu l-'imDaa' hunaa min faDliki.
mari:	tabxan.
'amiin 'al-maSrif:	sayyidatii, lam taktubii raqma jawaaz 'as-safar.

mari:	xafwan. lam 'arahu fii l-'istimaara. haa huwa.
'amiin 'al-maSrif:	shukran. tafaDDalii.
mari:	shukran jaziilan.

Mary: I would like to exchange dollars for dirhams.

Teller: How many dollars would you like to change?

Mary: $100, please.

Teller: Do you have a passport?

Mary: Yes. Here it is.

Teller: Thank you. How would you like the money?

Mary: Ten bills, please.

Teller: You need to sign here, please.

Mary: Of course.

Teller: Ma'am, you didn't write your passport number.

Mary: I'm sorry. I didn't see it on the form. Here it is.

Teller: Thank you. Here you go.

Mary: Thank you very much.